75

Jewish
Ceremonial
Embroidery

Kathryn Salomon

Jewish Ceremonial Embroidery

B. T. BATSFORD, LTD LONDON

ISBN 0 7314 52684

Typeset by Tameside Filmsetting, Ltd.
and printed in Great Britain by
The Bath Press
Bath, Somerset

for the publishers
B. T. Batsford Ltd
4 Fitzhardinge Street
London W1H 0AH

Contents

Acknowledgements

Many people have given their time and expertise to help me with this book and it is not possible to name them all. I would like to thank in particular my husband and friends, who have read and corrected the text in its various stages and have provided constructive criticism.

Some embroiderers have sent me photographs of their work and others have allowed me to photograph it, and I am very grateful. I would like to acknowledge the help of the following people and institutions who have given me information or allowed me to use photographs of items in their collections: Michael Keen of the Victoria & Albert Museum; the Jewish Museum, London; the Warburg Institute; Ruth Eis of the Judah Magnes Museum; Sylvia Herskowitz of the Yeshiva University Museum; Grace Cohen Grossman and Susanne Kester of the Hebrew Union College Skirball Museum; the State Jewish Museum of Prague and the Whitworth Art Gallery; the Verein für das Jüdische Museum der Schweiz; the Israel Museum; the Department of Antiquities of the Israel Ministry of Education and Culture; the Museum of the Chief Rabbinate, Hechal Shlomo; and Myron Schon of the Central Conference of American Rabbis. My thanks too to Ina Golub and Esther Carvalho for the information they gave me. I would also like to thank all the synagogues and private collectors who allowed me to photograph their possessions. Rachel Wright of Batsford guided me through this enterprise with calm professionalism and Judy Goldhill and Ian Ross provided additional photos. The vast majority of the photographic work for this book was undertaken by Dr Harold Rose who also gave enthusiastic support throughout.

Introduction

As a craftswoman I look backwards into history for inspiration and for the courage to produce exciting ideas for today. I feel that Jewish ceremonial embroidery should be a link between the past and the future. Avant-garde work can look incongruous when made for an object as ancient as the Torah scroll, and yet embroideries for the scroll must reflect our own times and culture to have true validity. A balance has to be achieved. So many of the traditional designs seen today in Jewish ceremonial art are little more than debased stereotypes; the whole area of Jewish symbolism needs to be reconsidered and revitalized. Exciting works are being produced today, examples of which are to be found in this book; these are part of our rich heritage and will prove to be a legacy for future generations. However, all those involved with Jewish ceremonial art, both patrons and craftspeople, need to put in time and effort to ensure a strong and vibrant tradition.

The craftsperson who produces embroideries for Jewish religious ceremonies needs to know the historical details of the Sanctuary, the Temple and the Synagogue. The background history of the Torah scroll and other religious artefacts, including the silver ornaments which decorate the scroll, need to be researched. This will help the embroiderer to avoid being coerced into conforming with unnecessary design restrictions. There is so much confusion on the supposed prohibition of figurative work that the embroiderer needs to know the facts in this very difficult area. There is a danger that if anything more than an abstract design is produced, some mistaken individual will say that the second commandment has been contravened. One needs to have one's arguments ready.

It is also helpful to know of the huge variation in the design of items in different parts of the world, both in the past and today. Materials, colours and designs have been and are very varied, and can be a rich source of ideas for the embroiderer.

In the past artists and craftspeople have been inspired to produce exciting contemporary pieces through looking at earlier periods. Sometimes their innovations have come about through misconceptions about the work from previous centuries. The neo-classical movement, for example, which swept through all the arts and crafts in Europe in the eighteenth century, was based upon the archaeological discoveries at Pompeii and also on some misconceptions about the art of ancient Greece and Rome. It really does not matter, because although craftspeople look backwards for inspiration, it is important to remember that we are not academics, and should not follow any past ideas slavishly. We should not make reproductions.

I hope that this does not sound too daunting. The aim of this book is to give the reader a glimpse of the rich Jewish heritage available so that it can be exploited to the full, and also to give the

Fig. 1 *Torah mantle; silk velvet and silk brocaded with silver, embroidered with silver-gilt and silver threads and coloured silks. Netherlands (Amsterdam) 1650–1700. (Victoria & Albert Museum, London.)*

embroiderer the weapons with which to reply to critics.

When I first started designing Jewish ceremonial embroideries I studied a magnificent Torah mantle in the Victoria and Albert Museum. Both its shape and design impressed me, and I resolved to produce something as beautiful and rich as the one before me. The mantle was made for a Sephardi synagogue and I come from an Ashkenazi background. Does it matter? The result was that I felt inspired; this is what counts.

chapter one

Jewish ceremonial embroidery through the ages

'This is my God and I will glorify Him' (Exodus 15:2) is taken by the rabbis as a command to make beautiful items in honour of God.

Here is the Talmudic answer to those who feel money, time and effort are better not spent on art and should be applied to more 'worthy' tasks: 'Make a beautiful Succah in His Honour, a beautiful lulav, a beautiful shofar, beautiful tzitzit, a beautiful Scroll of the Law, and write it with fine ink, a fine reed, a skilled scribe and wrap it about with beautiful silks.' (Shabbat 133b.)

If the very existence of Jewish ceremonial embroidery is justified by these quotations, the source of the symbolism and colours inherent in Jewish ceremonial embroidery is to be found in a particular passage in the Bible.

THE SANCTUARY IN THE DESERT

Chapters 25–8 of the book of Exodus describe the Sanctuary in the desert and the robes of the priests. This is the earliest documented evidence about embroidery among the Israelites. We return to it time and time again as the original source of symbols, colours and objects.

Here we learn of the four colours – blue, purple, scarlet and a colour referred to as linen – which are used symbolically for many items throughout Jewish history. Here we read of the high priest's robes, of his 'broidered coat' and the 'pomegranates of blue and

purple and scarlet round the hem and gold bells between them round about'. The ephod, the garment worn by the high priest over the blue robe, is described as being of 'gold, blue, purple and crimson yarn and of fine twisted linen, worked into designs'. Here too, the hangings of the Sanctuary are described as being of 'cunning' work with cherubim worked into them.

The seven-branched candlestick (the menorah) and other appurtenances which were used in the Sanctuary and later in the Temple, are also described. They have been used symbolically with great frequency by craftspeople over the ages. As the biblical style pares narrative and descriptive passages down to the bare essentials and never uses unnecessary words, the detailed descriptions indicate the great importance attached to the Sanctuary, its appurtenances and the people who made them.

THE ANCIENT HEBREWS

Both biblical descriptions and archaeological excavations from the period of Solomon, 973–933 BCE, show that the Hebrews were not as proficient as their neighbours in the crafts; Solomon had to import a court craftsman called Hiram from Tyre to construct the Temple. The passages describing Solomon's Temple in Kings and Chronicles are important as they mention the lavish amount of gold, the huge cherubim and the bronze sea supported by 12 bronze oxen which were used in the Temple.

Although no embroideries are described we know that they were highly prized in ancient times. Deborah's Song (Judges 5:30), approximately 1125 BCE, refers to embroidery as booty in war:

> A spoil of dyed garments of embroidery,
> Two dyed garments of broidery
> for the neck of every spoiler.

CONFLICTING ATTITUDES TOWARDS ART IN JUDAISM

Two groups with very different attitudes towards art appeared around the time of Solomon's Temple: a cultured, educated intelligentsia who appreciated aesthetics; and a group, epitomized by the prophets, who urged the people to return to a more austere religion, the religion of the desert.

Throughout Jewish history each of these attitudes has held sway at different times. It is not a question of one being more religious than the other; they are diametrically opposite points of view and the Jewish people have veered between them according to external circumstances.

DEFINITION OF JEWISH ART AND EMBROIDERY

The history of Jewish embroidery becomes more complicated by the time of the Babylonian Exile, 586 BCE. Jewish history is not a history of a nation in one land, except in very ancient times, and this is reflected in the development of Jewish ceremonial objects. It is the history of a people conquered on many occasions and dispersed in different lands. It is also the story of a people who *chose* to live in different countries from an early point in their history.

It is for these reasons that Jewish art and embroidery cannot be defined by national characteristics. All Jews, both ancient and modern, have been influenced by the art of their neighbours and by the dominant culture in which they have lived.

Since late antiquity the usual characteristics of a national art cannot be found in Jewish arts and crafts. From this period until the Emancipation in the eighteenth century it can be defined as the production of artefacts for religious purposes. After that time definition is more complex and the subject of debate between artists and historians. It is clear, however, that Jewish traditions and rituals differ all over the world and that there is no absolute Jewish style.

THE ORIGIN AND DEVELOPMENT OF THE SYNAGOGUE AND ITS APPURTENANCES

The synagogue is thought to have developed during the Babylonian Exile, when it is believed that 'By the rivers of Babylon' Jews gathered together to hear the words of the prophets. About a century and a half later Ezra the Scribe introduced regular readings from the Torah, the scrolls of the Law. These became a central part of synagogue ritual, which meant that each synagogue needed to own at least one copy of the Torah, and to have a suitable artefact in which to keep it.

The original synagogue also served as the courthouse, and it was thought not fitting to keep the sacred scrolls in the same room in which legal wrangles took place. It was for this reason that the scrolls were kept in a portable chest, called the Holy Ark after the Ark of the Covenant which contained the tablets of stone in the desert Sanctuary and in Solomon's Temple. II Chronicles 35:3 refers to the portable Ark in use at the time when Josiah restored the Temple.

Synagogues developed not only in the Diaspora, but also in the Holy Land itself, even in Jerusalem. It is believed that Psalm 74:8 refers to synagogues destroyed in Judea.

These facts are important for the craftsperson because they show the very long history of ceremonial items produced for the synagogue. They began to be used before the destruction of the Temple, both in the Holy Land and in the Diaspora.

THE INFLUENCE OF HELLENISM UPON JEWISH CEREMONIAL ARTEFACTS

Many Jews are taught about Hellenism as a culture with a philosophy in direct conflict with monotheism. The picture is not so clear-cut and Hellenic ideas of beauty affected the Jews just as they affected other peoples.

Alexander the Great introduced the Jews to Hellenism when he conquered Judea (334 BCE). He transported many Jews to his new city of Alexandria, where a prosperous community developed. They built a magnificent synagogue of which the rabbis said 'He who does not see it has not seen the glory of Israel.' (Talmud Sukkah 51b.) The synagogue was so vast that a flag had to be waved to inform the congregation when to respond.

Hellenistic influences as disseminated by the Romans can be seen not only in the developing love of beauty, but also in the shape of the synagogue. The assembly hall or basilica, common to all the towns of the Roman Empire, was the prototype for the early synagogue. The Temple itself, built by Herod, showed a Hellenic influence in its love of beauty and lavish decoration.

JEWISH EMBROIDERY AT THE TIME OF THE SECOND TEMPLE

Philo of Alexandria, who lived at the time of Agrippa (30 CE) and Josephus (first century CE) have both left us descriptions of the Temple built by Herod.

Josephus wrote of the 'Babylonian curtain' which separated the Holy of Holies from the rest of the Temple. The curtain probably contained rich-coloured appliqué and heavy gold fringes, typical of similar curtains used in contemporary Persian palaces. (It is hardly surprising that the curtain was of 'Babylonian' work, because of the influence of the large Babylonian diaspora.) The curtain was hung from a height of approximately 9 metres (29 ft). As it would have been far too heavy to pull aside if it was worked in one piece, it is reasonable to assume that it was made in two parts, with one design worked over the two halves. Such curtains were commonly used instead of doors throughout the Middle East. Archaeological excavations at Persepolis and Susa give some idea of how such curtains were hung. Similar ornate embroideries can also be glimpsed on stone reliefs from the time of Darius and Xerxes.

The Temple was a large employer of skilled labour. Masons, carpenters, weavers, embroiderers, goldsmiths, were all constantly employed in keeping the Temple and the royal palaces in good repair. Before Jerusalem fell in 70 CE, craftsmen and artisans lived and worked in specific areas with fellow-members of their own trades. They wore badges to denote their craft. Eleazar ben Azariah wrote, 'There is something grand about artisanship; every artisan boasts of his trade, grandly carrying his badge in the street.'

It seems that Jewish craftsmen may have come to Europe in the early years of the Common Era. It is said that a Jewish weaver called Baruch was called to Spain by a Roman prefect at the time of Herod.

JEWISH EMBROIDERY IN ROMAN TIMES

Jerusalem was still a city rich in crafts in post-biblical and Talmudic times. Many of the rabbis were themselves craftsmen. They formulated regulations for the dealings between craftspeople and their patrons from practical experience. These regulations (found in the Mishnah), influenced the Jewish craft guilds of seventeenth-century Poland.

Embroidery was considered a particularly desirable craft by the rabbis. It was praised by Rabbi Judah (Kiddushin 82a–b) as the most attractive because it was the cleanest.

Both Roman and Talmudic sources inform us of the superior textiles from Beth Shean in Judah. A Roman poet, Claudius Claudianus, who lived in the fourth century of the Common Era, wrote of textiles called *Judaica vela* which were manufactured in Egypt and had fantastic animals woven into them.

At this time skilled Jewish craftspeople practised their trades in many parts of the world. Informal guilds existed, some of which supported their own synagogues. It is also known that special areas were allocated in the Great Synagogue at Alexandria to the different crafts. At the same time, Jews were

אין כמוך באלהים יהוה ואין כמעשיך מלכותך מלכות כל עולמים יהוה מלך יהוה
ברוך המקום שנתן תורה לעמו ישראל ברוך הוא
אנכי יהוה אלהיך
לא יהיה לך
לא תשא את
זכור את יום
כבד את אביך
לא תרצח
לא תנאף
לא תגנב
לא תענה
לא תחמוד
קהלת יעקב

Fig. 2 *Ark curtain made of beadwork on a canvas ground; oriental, said to be Turkish, early eighteenth century. (Jewish Museum, London.)*

often members of the guilds in the nations in which they lived.

DEVELOPMENTS IN THE SYNAGOGUE BUILDING AND IN SYNAGOGUE RITUAL

Wherever the Jews lived they built synagogues. The early prototypes differed both in orientation and ritual from later models. They were constructed in such a way that prayers would rise through the doorway towards Jerusalem. At a later date the Holy Ark was carried into the prayer hall and placed against the eastern wall. In the Talmud (Sota 39b) worshippers are warned not to leave the prayer hall until the scrolls of the Law have been carried out. The next stage was for the Ark to be kept permanently against the wall which faced towards Jerusalem (obviously this was not always the eastern wall).

It can therefore be seen that the most sacred item in the synagogue, the Holy Ark, has changed considerably in shape, size and location over the ages. The items associated with it, such as the embroideries, and the embroideries for the Torah scroll, have also changed.

JEWISH CRAFTS UNDER ISLAM

Jews were allowed to work in many different occupations and trades in ancient Byzantium. By the twelfth century they were exceptionally skilled in all aspects of the silk trade. When Norman crusaders captured Corinth and Thebes in 1147, they took the best silk workers back to Sicily to establish the silk industry at Palermo (as recorded by Benjamin of Tudela – see below). There were many Jews amongst them. Skilled craftsmen, both Jews and non-Jews, were also captured and brought back from Corfu and other centres.

When the Arabs crossed the Straits of Gibraltar in 711 and conquered Spain, the same culture and language was dominant from Baghdad to the foot of the Pyrenees. After initial fanaticism, the Muslims were tolerant of the Jews who followed them as traders, craftsmen and peasants all over their empire.

Benjamin of Tudela, who travelled all over the Islamic world between 1165 and 1173, through Italy, Greece, Constantinople, the Archipelago, Cyprus, Antioch, Palestine, Damascus, Baghdad, Persia, India, Ceylon, Egypt and perhaps even China, noted particulars of all the Jewish communities he encountered during his travels. He wrote of Jews working as tanners, glass-makers and embroiderers, and of the major role Jews played in the silk industry. (The silk industry was of major economic importance at this time and fantastic prices were paid for single pieces.)

Contemporary sources, such as Benjamin and Pethaia, wrote of the fabulously embroidered textiles worn by the Exilarch (the governer of the Jewish community in the Babylonian Exile). Seder Olam Zuta described the 'gorgeous silver coverings, and coverings in blue, purple and scarlet red' of the wooden canopy prepared for the Sabbath of the inauguration of the Exilarch in Baghdad. Baghdad was famous for its crafts in the Middle Ages and the craftsmen obviously wanted to display their skills.

THE CAIRO GENIZA

In Judaism, when documents bearing the name of God are no longer of use (usually prayer books) they are not destroyed, but buried in a cemetery. Items are usually accumulated until the quantity merits interment. Oriental Jewish communities store the items in a room called a *Geniza* until burial. A unique Geniza was discovered in Fustat (old Cairo) which contained many civil as well as religious documents. They give us a unique picture of the life of Jews in Egypt, the Holy Land, Tunisia and Sicily from the eleventh to the thirteenth centuries. The documents survived because of the very dry air of the region and because the Geniza had never been emptied.

17

Egyptian Gold-thread Embroiderers

We learn from the Geniza fragments that some crafts were predominantly Jewish. This was true of embroidery, particularly gold-thread embroidery. Jewish women worked in the palaces upon commissions for members of the princely houses. The rabbis were concerned about the length of time the women had to work in a Muslim environment, but they argued that they had their husbands' permission, and that they needed the income. (Later, Jewish women embroiderers worked in the Egyptian palaces from 1500 to 1800. Rabbi David Ben Simra ruled that such work was permissible so long as the women were over 40, accompanied by two other women, and did not work at one table with the men!)

Organization of the crafts

The crafts were organized into small groups, usually family units run by a single craftsman, but sometimes a clan and occasionally a partnership with no more than five partners.

The craftsmen preferred to be self-employed, but sometimes the most skilled were forced to work in government textile factories.

Craftsmanship was held in high esteem, and some of the crafts were predominantly Jewish. This was the case with goldsmithing and embroidery, both of which had their own guilds at Fez. These associations were much looser organizations than the later Christian craft guilds in the Middle Ages.

Early records of Torah mantles and Torah ornaments

A Geniza fragment dated 1185–7 mentions Torah crowns and finials and 22 Torah covers, some of them brocaded with gold. There are no surviving Torah ornaments or embroideries from this period, so the information is of great importance.

SPANISH JEWRY

The period when the Moors ruled Spain was a 'golden age' for Jews. They practised occupations ranging from diplomacy and medicine to all the handicrafts. Files of notaries in Barcelona show that Jews were highly skilled embroiderers in both silk and gold. Jewish lacemarkers worked in Barcelona, Toledo and Mallorca. Some of their products were interwoven with gold and silver threads and were so costly that sumptuary laws had to be passed.

All this changed with the supremacy of Christianity, and in 1391 persecution began. Mobs annihilated whole communities, synagogues were confiscated and turned into churches, Jews who refused to accept forcible baptism were expelled from Spain. As the Jews and the Moors were the most highly skilled craftspeople in Spain at this time, the crafts suffered with their expulsion. The refugees settled throughout the Ottoman Empire, all along the North African and around the Mediterranean coasts. They outdid the local Jewish communities in numbers and by dint of their superior education. Although they brought their trade secrets with them and enriched the communities and countries in which they now lived, they clung to their Spanish traditions and customs.

Some Jews did not leave Spain; those who had accepted enforced conversion stayed on as New Christians or 'Conversos'. Their neighbours called them 'Marranos' (said to mean 'swine'). The Marranos were highly educated, wealthy and influential. From the seventeenth century they formed communities in Holland and England and openly reverted to Judaism. These communities built beautiful synagogues and commissioned sumptuous embroideries for them. (An example is Bevis Marks Synagogue in London.)

DEFINITION OF SEPHARDI, ASHKENAZI AND ROMANIOTE JEWS

The Jews who came from Spain and Portugal came to be known as 'Sephardim' (which comes from the medieval Hebrew for Spain). Their customs, the manner in which they dress the Sifrei Torah, the names of the items in the synagogue, their foods, dialect, and even their Hebrew script differ from those of the Jews who came from Central and Eastern Europe. These Jews are known as 'Ashke-

Fig. 3 *Ark in a private collection containing one Torah scroll with silver rollers covered in a silk Torah mantle and two tikkim. (This would be very unusual in a synagogue Ark; one would have the scrolls either clothed in mantles or enclosed in tikkim.) One of the tikkim has a velvet cover, the other is covered with metal. According to the owner, the distinction between the two materials is purely one of cost.*

nazim' (medieval Hebrew for Germany). Today, the term 'Sephardi' has come to mean any Jew who is not an Ashkenazi, but this is not correct.

The most ancient group of Jews are the Romaniote Jews. They trace their history from Alexandria in the Hellenistic Diaspora, through the Byzantine Empire to Constantinople, the Balkans and Asia Minor. In Greece there were separate Sephardi and Romaniote communities until World War Two.

Both Sephardi and Ashkenazi Jews clothe the Sifrei Torah in mantles, but they use different shapes, materials and colours. Romaniote Jews keep the scrolls in round wooden cases which are known as *tikkim*.

Jews who lived under Muslim rule have always practised crafts, in contrast to the Jews of Central and Eastern Europe, principally Ashkenazim, for whom such skills were proscribed for many centuries. Attitudes towards these trades differed substantially between the two groups: craftsmanship has always been highly regarded amongst Jews who lived under Muslim rule, but even when the Central and Eastern European Jews were allowed to practise crafts again, they considered them to be lowly occupations.

Pinkas ha-Medina, when discussing the education of orphans, wrote 'Boys to whom God has granted wisdom that their study will be a success should be induced to study Torah at school: boys whose abilities are not sufficient for study of the Torah shall be induced to take service or to learn the works of some crafts.'

INFLUENCE OF THE CRUSADES

There are only a handful of artefacts which have survived from before 1500. One of the reasons for this is the continual cycle of persecution, confiscation of property and expulsion which affected community after community. When the Jews were driven into exile, they were not allowed to take anything of value with them.

Mary Eirwen Jones, in *A History of Western Embroidery*, describes the Crusaders setting forth in medieval armour and returning home weighed down with luxurious embroidered materials, the like of which had never been seen in Europe. They had, of course, pillaged them from Muslims and Jews. On their way to the Crusades, the Crusaders sacked and looted all the Jewish communities they passed.

JEWISH CRAFTS IN CENTRAL AND EASTERN EUROPE UNTIL THE EMANCIPATION

The history of arts and crafts is usually divided into the Medieval period, the Renaissance and the Baroque. These divisions do not apply to Jewish arts and crafts. Apart from the paucity of material before the sixteenth century, we have to acknowledge the fact that the Jews, shut up in their ghettos, encountered change and relinquished styles at a slower rate than the outside world. The high points of influence which excited artists and craftspeople filtered through gradually and were very slowly accepted.

For Jews, the great divisions are the period of isolation in the ghettos, and the period after the Emancipation, when the ghetto walls came down and the Jewish people were flooded with new ideas and accepted into the outside world.

Italy

When the Jews first came to Europe they practised crafts alongside their pagan and Christian brethren. This continued until the thirteenth century when the Christian craft guilds gradually forced them out of every honourable occupation in most of Europe. This was not true in Italy, where some crafts had been practised since antiquity and were known as Jewish occupations. Amongst these, alongside goldsmithing and ceramics, were lacemaking and embroidery.

Poland

In Poland too, Jews managed to withstand guild pressure for a long time. In the mid-thirteenth century, the king introduced a policy of attracting German traders and craftsmen to form a new middle class, and in spite of persecution and massacres, the Jews were, for a time, more fortunate than their compatriots elsewhere in Christian Europe. Restrictions gradually increased and from the sixteenth century the Polish nobility and the rising middle classes pushed the Jews out of commerce. They turned in increasing numbers to crafts, and by the second half of the seventeenth century more than half the Jewish artisans worked in the clothing industry.

Many of the items were produced solely for the Jewish market, but embroiderers in Poland produced work for Jew and Gentile. They made the famous silver and gold intertwined belts worn by Polish noblemen. Polish Torah mantles were made from these belts. There are records of one Bezalel, son of Nathan, who was commissioned to make 'Turkish' curtains for the king. By the seventeenth century there were many Jewish craft guilds and apprentices included both boys and girls.

Decline of Polish Jewry – development of folk art
1648 was a crucial year for Jews all over Europe: the Cossacks, led by Chmelnitzki, broke up the Jewish communities in Poland. The now impoverished Polish Jews were unable to take part in the artistic developments which took place amongst Jewish communities elsewhere in Europe. However, they developed a rich and distinctive form of decoration for their synagogues. A striking style of wooden synagogue developed in Poland with the interior completely covered with elaborate paintings. These were produced by itinerant artists. Hangings and embroideries were designed and produced for the synagogue and signed by their makers. Often travelling scribes designed them and laid out the lettering.

Bohemia and Moravia

The richest source of antique Jewish embroideries is the State Jewish Museum at Prague, which was greatly enhanced during World War Two. The Nazis thought that the assembled religious artefacts of all the Jewish communities of Czechoslovakia (Jews had lived in Prague since the time of Charlemagne) would prove an interesting reminder of an extinct people. Today, the magnificent textile collection of over 10,000 items allows historians to research textile history as well as the history of Jewish

Fig. 4 *Kapporet, Moravia, Brno 1740; velvet with silver thread embroidery.* (State Jewish Museum Prague; photo: Whitworth Art Gallery, Manchester.)

ceremonial textiles and the history of the Jews of Moravia and Bohemia.

The museum possesses the earliest extant Torah curtain. It is signed and dated by Solomon Perlsticker and his wife Golda, who presented it in 1590. Two years later their son Pinhas and daughter-in-law Gautel added further embellishments and signed and dated it too.

The Jewish custom of embroidering an inscription upon each item donated to the synagogue has proved of immense value historically. If in general we would rather not see a curtain or other item with 'donated by . . . in memory of . . .' worked in large letters upon it, we must bear in mind that this practice has enabled historians to build up a fascinating historical picture of the community in these areas. Textile historians have been able to refer to the inscriptions when researching the development of styles and fabrics. There is obvious merit in continuing the tradition of personal inscriptions, but perhaps they could be used a little more discreetly.

Vestments belonging to the museum show that 'Perlhefter' and 'Perlsticker' were familiar names in

the Bohemian Jewish community. They both refer to the skill of bead embroidery or bead stitchery, which attained a very high level in Bohemia during the fourteenth century, and was practised in the Prague ghetto long after it had declined elsewhere.

Another characteristic which is revealed through research in the collection is the incorporation of precious fabrics, often antique, into synagogue vestments. It is probable that the Jewish merchants imported rare brocades as well as spices from the Middle East. Certainly antique pieces were valued, cherished and incorporated into the synagogue furnishings and were refurbished again and again.

The use of renovated fabrics in synagogue vestments

An Italian doctor, Barnardin Ramazzini, Professor of Medicine at the University of Padua, in a treatise on the Diseases of Artisans in 1700, commented

> Nearly all Jews, especially the lower classes to which most of them belong, are employed in work at which they must sit or stand. They are mostly given to sewing and refurbishing old clothes – the women above all, whether married or single make their living by needlework. . . . At this they excel and are so expert that they can join and mend garments of wool, silk or any other material so that the seam is quite invisible . . .

21

This ability to refurbish old fabrics was used by Jews all over Europe and can be seen in many Torah mantles and parochot in museums. They are often made from the clothing of the rich which has been cut up and remade. The skill which the workers acquired with old clothes they adapted, whenever possible, to the making up of new fabrics.

From the fifteenth century the numbers of Jews employed in the crafts greatly increased in Bohemia, Moravia, Poland, Lithuania and Austria.

The very frequency of the rulings by the craft guilds against Jews at this time provides evidence that the rules cannot have been working effectively. Jewish craft guilds were formed in Prague, Moravia and Poland. A drawing of a procession of the Jewish Guilds of Embroiderers and Tailors in Prague in 1741 can be seen in *The Synagogue Treasures of Bohemia and Moravia* by Hana Volavkana. The contemporary Christian guilds had far stricter rules; they had become rigid and exploited their workers. Despite hindrance, journeymen worked for the Jews and taught them their trades. The Jewish craftsmen and women, unfettered by the inflexible guild rules, proved sharp competitors.

JEWISH CEREMONIAL EMBROIDERY IN THE SEVENTEENTH AND EIGHTEENTH CENTURIES

Magnificent Jewish ceremonial embroideries were produced during the seventeenth and for much of the eighteenth centuries. The reasons for this flowering were:

1 If 1648 marked the start of the decline of Polish Jewish communities, it also marked the beginning of affluence for Jews in Germany and elsewhere in Central Europe. The Peace of Westphalia, signed in 1648, terminated the Thirty Years War in Germany. Trade resumed and the communities in Vienna and Bavaria became wealthy.

The Marranos began to settle in Holland in 1590, and the community flourished when Amsterdam became an important centre for world trade. Ashkenazi communities, too, grew up in the Netherlands from 1620. These wealthy communities kept in touch with each other and with the new community of Sephardi Jews which was established in England in 1656.

2 The wealthy Jewish merchants, particularly in the Catholic countries, saw their neighbours' magnificent churches with splendid Baroque altars and decorations, and wanted to emulate them. They wished to spend their wealth on art, just like their non-Jewish neighbours, and at this stage chose Jewish ceremonial art. At the same time, they were afraid to show their wealth to the outside world, and therefore commissioned portable religious items for the home and synagogue.

3 The heavy restrictions which had regulated the size and height of synagogues during much of the Middle Ages were gradually repealed and it was now possible to consider larger, more elegant buildings.

4 The Baroque period, with its lavish use of gold, seemed to recall the style of the Sanctuary in the desert and Solomon's Temple in Jerusalem. It was a style which seemed natural and comfortable to the Jews and lent itself to the elaborate embroideries produced at this time.

5 The increasing use of printed books had a number of effects upon Jewish arts and crafts. Firstly, illuminated manuscripts had long been a craft in which Jews had excelled, but the development of printing made it obsolete. Those who wished to collect art, or to practise it, had to turn to other art forms. Secondly, the printed book spread ideas at a much faster rate than had been possible before, and the artistic developments of the Renaissance and Baroque masters were increasingly available to both the Jewish artists and their patrons.

Jewish embroiderers of the seventeenth and eighteenth centuries

There were a number of expert embroiderers, both men and women, who were active during this period.

We know of two Italian craftswomen because they both signed their work. Rachel, the wife of Leone Montefiore, worked and signed a parokhet from Ancona dated 1630. A splendid curtain, now in the possession of the Jewish Museum, New York, was embroidered by Magdalena Bassan in 1738 for the synagogue in Padua.

Records show that Johann Sebastian Stein was a court embroiderer in Mainz, Germany, in 1725. As happened so often, particularly at this time, he converted to Christianity to achieve recognition.

In 1738 an elaborate embroidered cover for the tomb of the Emperor Heinrich and his wife Kunigunde in the cathedral at Bamberg, Germany, was worked by Gerson Mayer.

We also know that a Bohemian Jew embroidered Catholic vestments in Fulda in southern Germany in the eighteenth century and that he was highly skilled in gold embroidery.

Two Bavarian craftsmen produced magnificent parochot during this period. Elkone Naumburg produced work for the Augsburg and Hildesheim synagogues and another curtain owned by the Hambro synagogue in London was probably made by him. The Ashkenazi Dutch community refused one of his parochot which they had previously commissioned because they found it too elaborate. The Jewish Museum, New York, possesses a parokhet and valance by another famous Bavarian embroiderer, Jacob Koppel Gans.

Decline of Jewish ceremonial embroidery

The standards of excellence achieved in all areas of lavish ceremonial art declined towards the end of the eighteenth century. As the outside world became more sympathetic to Jews they gradually became involved in the mainstream of European civilization. At first it was only the wealthy court Jew who was affected, but after the French Revolution the ghetto walls were dismantled all over Europe and Jews were given equal rights with their neighbours.

Aesthetes wanted to emulate their Gentile neighbours and collect painting and sculpture instead of religious artefacts. Artists, too, wished to explore all the artistic disciplines and address themselves to secular themes rather than to producing religious objects. The vestments from this period are in general of a lower standard than earlier pieces.

THE NINETEENTH CENTURY

The Emancipation was not the only reason for the deterioration; craftsmanship generally declined in many areas because of the Industrial Revolution.

Fig. 5 *Velvet kippah; silk and metal thread embroidery from Wangen (Lake Constance), end of the nineteenth century.* (Verein für das Jüdische Museum der Schweiz.)

The nineteenth century was a period of great experimentation in synagogue architecture, but vestments seem to have remained very much in the spirit of the Baroque, which had such a dominant influence on Jewish ceremonial art. Embroiderers did not take up the challenge of the new architectural developments in the synagogue.

Aesthetics suffered from another problem during this century. Simplicity was equated with poverty and this belief led to excessive lavishness in the interior design of synagogues. Some professional houses continued to produce work of a very high quality: one Victor Abrahams was embroiderer to Queen Victoria. However, the general erosion of craftsmanship continued, with the traditional goldwork techniques being replaced by cruder methods.

A wealth of embroidered pieces for domestic use can be found dating from the nineteenth century. Some are privately owned, often made by relatives, and many are in public collections. This seems to have been the period when the kippah began to be popular (although its greatest popularity came about in the twentieth century).

THE TWENTIETH CENTURY

If one looks in synagogues and homes at the embroideries made in the first part of this century, one is forced to admit that the general standard was very low.

Reasons for the decline of Jewish ceremonial embroidery in the twentieth century

1 The legacy of the Industrial Revolution caused a decline in the quality of much craftwork.

2 When the great wave of emigrants left Russia for Britain and the United States in the 1880s, they had to struggle so hard to make a living that they put aesthetic considerations to one side.

3 The children of the emigrants were determined to enter into the cultural environment of the wider community, and in doing so, lost much of their Jewish heritage. (The two world wars did much to aid assimilation and loosen cultural and religious bonds.)

4 The Victorian attitude to embroidery as an occupation for ladies to pursue at home has been the cause of a negative attitude towards embroidery as a craft.

Reasons for the revival of Jewish ceremonial embroidery

1 Recent history, in the form of the Holocaust, has taught all Jews that it is impossible to become totally assimilated.

2 The State of Israel has generated great pride amongst Jews all over the world. In Israel there has been a revival of interest in Jewish art. The Bezalel Academy in Jerusalem has trained Jewish artists throughout much of this century. The Centre for Jewish Art at the Hebrew University of Jerusalem studies Jewish Art and publishes material about it. Many museums in Israel display Jewish religious artefacts to great effect, mount special exhibitions and publish special works.

3 In the United States, architects have designed exciting synagogues and used bold modern embroideries in the interiors. Books and exhibitions about Jewish ceremonial embroidery have stimulated the public and the craftspeople.

4 In Britain, the renaissance of ecclesiastical embroideries cannot have failed to have an effect upon Jewish embroideries. Very simply, it has become easier today to find help and advice in making Jewish ceremonial work because of the great interest in ecclesiastical embroidery. Exhibitions show the interested embroiderer the variety of styles and techniques which can be adopted. Today, as in the past, Jewish ceremonial embroiderers are greatly influenced by the styles and techniques used by their compatriots of different religions.

5 There is an increasing interest generally in skilled craftsmanship.

6 The Women's Liberation Movement has taken up embroidery as an art form which is peculiarly feminine. Judy Chicago has produced a major work, 'The Dinner Party', which specifically uses embroidery as one of its media because it is a 'women's craft'. Women who are not militant feminists are still affected by some of the attitudes the movement espouses.

All these diverse sources have breathed new life into an ancient craft. There is an ever-increasing interest in Jewish ceremonial embroidery today.

chapter two

Figurative art and the synagogue

The question of whether figurative art is permissible in embroidery for the synagogue is a problematic one. A thorough evaluation is needed of the changing Jewish attitudes in the past, so that the embroiderer who wishes to use figurative designs has enough relevant information to be able to argue the case.

Exodus 20:4 and Deuteronomy 4:16–18 expressly forbid the making of 'any likeness of what is in the heavens above or on the earth below, or in the waters under the earth'. However, many rabbis throughout the ages have ruled that this refers to the making of graven images for the purpose of worshipping them, *not* to using them for decoration.

Jewish attitudes to the use of figurative art in places of public worship have varied considerably throughout history. We know that there were golden cherubim both in the Sanctuary in the desert and in Solomon's Temple. In the case of the latter, there were two gilded olive-wood cherubim, approximately 5 metres (16 ft) high, in the Holy of Holies and alternating carved and gilt cherubim and palm trees surrounding the main hall. The cherubim were probably composite figures with lion-like bodies, human heads and wings. Other items in the Temple also incorporated figurative art: the huge 'molten sea' was supported by twelve bronze oxen (I Kings 7:23–6).

During the time of the Roman occupation of Judah there is some evidence of figurative art in Jerusalem. However, Josephus wrote in *Antiquities* XVIII, 8:2 that the Jews rose in rebellion when Caligula tried to install a statue of himself in the Temple. This is hardly surprising. Emperor worship was the official Roman religion, and the Jews were constantly rebelling against the heavy yoke of Rome; they rose in revolt when the Roman eagle or the Roman standard were placed in the Temple. Josephus gave the Second Commandment as the reason, but political considerations are probably more realistic.

In the early years of the Common Era we find that the Talmudic rabbis in Babylonia seems to have made no objection to a statue of the king being placed in the synagogue of Nehardea (Babylonia Talmud, Avodah Zarah 43b, Rosh Hashanah 24b.) In this case there was no question of idolatory as the Babylonians were not pagan, and moreover there was no question of oppression of the Jewish people.

The Palestinian Talmud states: 'In the days of Rabbi Johanan they began to paint on the walls, and he did not prevent them. In the days of Rabbi Abun they began to make designs on mosaics and he did not prevent them' (Avodah Zarah 41a).

Frescoes and mosaics containing biblical narrative, animals and Temple symbols have been found in the excavations of the Dura Europos and Beth Alpha synagogues. In the case of the frescoes from Dura Europos, even the Hand of God was included. It is also probable that stone lions flanked the Torah-shrine at Beth Alpha.

Throughout the centuries Jews have been influenced by their neighbours' attitudes to figurative art. They were anxious to avoid any risk of being accused of pagan idol worship. If they were able to live unmolested there was often a more lenient attitude to figurative art, but when they were being persecuted they became more iconoclastic.

Fig. 6 *Torah mantle of crimson velvet with metal thread embroidery showing the figures of Moses (carrying the scroll) and Aaron, 1764. (Jewish Museum, London; copyright Warburg Institute.)*

The very rigorous attitudes of Islam to figurative art had a deep effect upon the Jews who lived under its rule, and they became increasingly negative about the use of animal and human figures in decoration.

The personal attitudes of different rabbis also affected their congregation's attitude towards figurative art, and the rabbinic rulings which have been handed down over the ages. The famous rabbi Maimonides, who lived in twelfth-century Egypt, used to close his eyes whilst praying in the synagogue so as not to be disturbed by images on

the embroideries which hung there. However, he ruled that painted, embroidered or woven human images were permissible. He felt that sculpted images should not be allowed, 'lest fools be misled by them and think they are for the purpose of idolatory. . . .'

Differing attitudes to figurative art can be seen in twelfth-century Europe. Rabbi Ephraim ben Isaac of Regensburg ruled that it was quite permissible to use textiles containing birds, fish and horses in the synagogue as animal worship was no longer a problem. During the same century Rabbi Eliakim ben Joseph wanted to remove stained-glass windows containing animal designs from the Cologne Synagogue.

Simon Achevolti, who died in 1609, was worried that the citizens of Venice would accuse the Ashkenazi community of worshipping the trees and plants which decorated their synagogue.

As the wider world became less hostile and the Jews emerged from the ghettos they adopted the forms and customs of their neighbours more freely. During the seventeenth and eighteenth centuries, the human form was depicted on Torah breastplates (usually the figures of Moses and Aaron), Torah mantles, spice boxes and chanukiot, on parochot (here animal and human forms were often incorporated into the coats of arms of the donors of the parokhet) and even on gravestones.

The famous Polish wooden synagogues of this period were completely covered with murals throughout their interiors. Plants, animals, fantastic creatures, human beings jostled against one another all over the walls, the ceiling and even the Ark.

The custom of dedicating an embroidered Torah binder at the birth of a boy in German communities, especially during the nineteenth century, also shows the use of the human figure. People were often embroidered upon the binders, holding up the Torah scroll or standing beneath the wedding canopy.

In the twentieth century there are modern synagogues in the United States which have incorporated the human figure not only into murals in the vestibule of the synagogue, but also on the Ark doors themselves.

Present Sephardi opinion suggests that neither animal nor human forms are acceptable in the modern Sephardi synagogue. However, they were certainly acceptable in the past as can be seen from rabbinic rulings. (See Maimonides above.)

CONCLUSION

The changes of attitude across the centuries have been discussed and we must now consider where this leaves the modern embroiderer who wishes to produce work for the synagogue. No definitive answer can be given. The one point which does become clear when the historical background is examined is that attitudes vary; opinions differ from century to century and from community to community. This must be the contemporary embroiderer's guide. The most cautious approach is never to use the human figure. However, if some human forms are inherent in the proposed design, the embroiderer should proceed only after consulting the rabbi of the congregation for whom the work is intended.

One must also bear in mind that British congregations tend to be more traditional than those in the United States. Photographs show that the human figure has been used in Progressive synagogues in the States, but I have never seen it used in Britain.

Animal forms are usually acceptable in most Ashkenazi congregations. They have been used in both traditionally Orthodox and Progressive synagogues all over the world in ancient and modern times.

For a fuller discussion of the subject read *No Graven Image* by Joseph Gutman.

RELIGIOUS RESTRICTIONS UPON MATERIALS

Leviticus 19:19 and Deuteronomy 22:11 specifically proscribe the combination of linen and wool for items worn by Jews. This mixture is called *shatnes* and is one of the reasons so many Jews have been involved in the textile and clothing trades over the ages. (Religious Jews wanted to ensure that their clothing was shatnes free.)

Fig. 7 *Torah binder, linen; detail with a figure holding a scroll. (*Hebrew Union College Skirball Museum, Los Angeles.*)*

ולחופה

Fig. 8 *Torah binder, linen, Germany 1719. Detail showing figures beneath a chuppah (wedding canopy).* (Hebrew Union College Skirball Museum, Los Angeles.)

Contemporary orthodox Jews in London who wish to ensure that their clothing complies with these laws consult Rabbi Royde of the Shatnes Research Institute. He gave me the following explanation of which materials are permissible for Jewish ceremonial embroidery.

The use of linen and wool is forbidden for garments, and one has therefore to define clearly what a garment is. The *Shulchan Aruch* YD 301 (a commentary on the Talmud), states that shatnes cannot be used in a curtain of soft material as one might wrap oneself in it. The mixture is permissible in a coarse fabric. Elsewhere in the *Shulchan Aruch*, the rabbis rule that a parokhet may contain shatnes as it is a permanent fixture, and no one would use this holy article as a shawl. This ruling does not apply to the use of linen and wool in smaller ceremonial embroideries such as Torah mantles, as they can be wrapped over the arm.

Any item made for a synagogue should comply with these laws, and many Jews would prefer items for their own personal religious use to comply with them too.

Great care needs to be taken when choosing backing materials and interlinings, as they can contain linen. One cannot use a linen backing or interlining and then use felt for padding areas of embroidery as felt contains wool. It is usually possible to find alternative materials for all the occasions when linen might be used.

chapter three

Symbolism

The symbols used for Jewish religious purposes have changed more than is generally realized over the centuries. The very earliest symbols were not those we necessarily associate most with Judaism today, and some of the most common contemporary symbols possess neither a particularly Jewish pedigree, nor a lengthy Jewish history.

This can be a positive factor as it gives the embroiderer great freedom. The symbols used over the ages are so numerous and diverse that we can use ancient ones to make new and exciting designs and overcome modern clichés.

CHERUBIM

Exodus 25–8, the description of the Sanctuary in the desert and its appurtenances, is most important as a source of ancient symbolism. The cherubim which flanked the Ark of the Covenant mentioned in this passage were probably influenced by Phoenician and Syrio-Hittite art. We have some idea of their appearance from the remains of Ahab's ivory house

diagram 1 *Phoenician ivory, ninth–eighth century* BCE *from the British Museum.*

(876–853 BCE). In all probability they were composite figures with the body of a lion, the head of a man and two wings. Similar beings are described by Ezekiel in his vision. His creatures possessed the heads of men and eagle's wings. They were probably influenced by the huge stone figures which guarded the Assyrian palaces. (Examples of these statues, and the ivories from Ahab's ivory house, can be found in the British Museum.) When the cherubim were used symbolically in later times they were often shown in embroideries as two wings or abstract figures.

THE MENORAH

The seven-branched candlestick known as the *menorah* is also described in great detail in the above passage. It was also an important item in the Temple. After the destruction of the Temple it was probably the most important Jewish symbol and symbolized the Temple itself for the Jewish people.

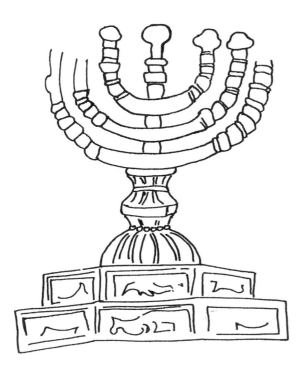

diagram 2 *The Temple menorah as depicted on the Arch of Titus in Rome.*

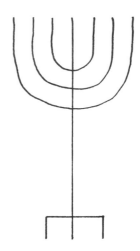

diagram 3 *Menorah as depicted in the Roman catacombs.*

Although the rabbis forbade the representation of the Temple menorah in synagogues, it can be seen on ancient synagogue floor mosaics and in frescoes and was used with great frequency in the Roman catacombs and on Roman gilt glass. A representation of the Temple menorah can be seen on the Arch of Titus in Rome. The Jewish captives are shown carrying the Temple appurtenances in a triumphal procession.

The menorah has been portrayed in many different styles over the ages. The bases of the menorot in Roman catacombs frequently resembled three-pronged forks. Modern menorot are often starkly simple. A Holocaust memorial in the form of a wooden menorah in the vestibule of the Stanmore Synagogue, Middlesex, is made of seven simple wooden columns fixed to the wall behind a glass table which is also wall mounted.

The mystical element in Judaism has associated the menorah with Psalm 67 which was written along its branches. *The Golden Menorah*, published in the sixteenth century in Prague, said that the words of Psalm 67, 'May God be gracious to us and bless us, and cause his face to shine upon us', were used by King David upon his shield together with a depiction of the menorah. This, rather than the six-pointed star, appears to have been David's emblem. (See *diagram 2*.)

Fig. 9 *Ark curtain depicting the Temple and the menorah. New West End Synagogue, London. Designed by Alfred Cohen and embroidered by the Royal School of Needlework.*

Other associations with the menorah are that it is a stylized Tree of Life or that it symbolizes the Burning Bush.

Fig. 10 *Menorah, detail of* fig. 9.

Fig. 11 *An arm of the menorah in* fig. 9.

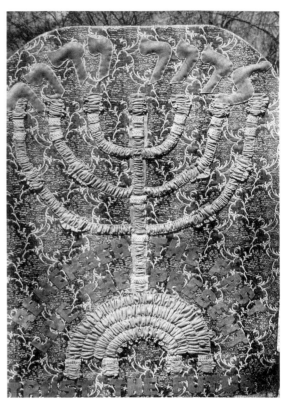

Fig. 12 *'From generation to generation'; soft sculpture by Francine Fierstein and Sylvia Wolff (Scarsdale and Tarrytown, New York). Ultra suede and damask, 112 × 127 cm (44 × 50 in.).* (Private collection.)

THE HOLY ARK – THE ARON HA-KODESH

After the destruction of the Temple new symbolism appeared in Jewish ceremonial art. The Holy Ark (the Torah-shrine, the receptacle for the Torah, the scrolls of the Law) appeared as a major symbol in the catacombs, in mosaics, on bowls, on oil lamps and so forth.

The mosaic floors of ancient synagogues show the Ark flanked by two lions and two menorot, together with symbols from the Temple, the priestly jug and ewer, and symbols of the festivals such as the ram's horn (the *shofar* which is used for the New Year and Day of Atonement), the symbols of the harvest festival Succot (the *lulav* and *etrog*), clusters of grapes and the kiddush cup.

Fig. 13 *Detail of* fig. 9: *the Temple.*

It is interesting to see how symbolism has changed over the ages. Ancient Jewish art often depicted the Akedah (the story of the binding of Isaac) and the zodiac. Neither of these symbols is very popular today. The meaning of some symbols seems to have been lost even in ancient times. Researches on the frescoes of the Dura Europos Synagogue (third century CE) reveal that specific colours and symbols were worn by men and others by women. By the time of the Ravenna mosaics (540 CE) the original meaning was lost and they were used purely for decoration.

TEMPLE APPURTENANCES

Images of incense burners, shovels, the altar, the table of shew bread, trumpets, jugs and ewers as well as symbols for the priests have all been used throughout the ages. They appeared with great frequency upon the valances for the Ark (see *Figs 44, 51*).

Fig. 14 *Torah mantle; brocade in gold and silver thread and coloured silks. Metal thread embroidery, detail showing an open Ark with a scroll. (For complete mantle, see fig. 65.) (Spanish and Portuguese Jews Congregation, London.)*

SYMBOLS OF THE COHANIM AND LEVITES

The use of hands raised in the specific manner used for the priestly benediction has proved popular in the past, but it has recently fallen from favour. Sometimes, when items were donated to the synagogues by Levites or Cohanim, the appropriate symbols, jug and ewer for the Levites, hands raised in priestly benediction for Cohanim, were incorporated in the embroidery.

Fig. 15 *Challah cover; velvet and silk with metal thread embroidery, depicting the table of shew bread. 1902. (Private collection.)*

Fig. 16 *Torah mantle; velvet, early twentieth century. The design shows the three crowns of the Law, the Priesthood and the Monarchy, and the hands of a priest raised in benediction. (Property of a Yeshiva in London.)*

diagram 4 *The lions rampant each side of the crown of the Law, and the jug and ewer, symbol of the Levites, from a nineteenth century parokhet.*

TWISTED COLUMNS

There is an ancient tradition that the two columns called Yakhin and Boaz, which stood in front of the Temple of Solomon, were twisted columns and that they were taken to St Peter's in Rome. It was for this reason that they were used so often in designs of the seventeenth and eighteenth centuries. (The twisted shape was, of course, very sympathetic to Baroque taste.)

The twisted columns in all probability do originate from St Peter's, but may well come from those used by Bernini in the canopy over the altar (1624–33). They appeared on the Ark, on parochot, Torah mantles, breastplates and on the title pages of books. (It is likely that they were first used in illustrations in books and then copied for synagogue art.) The very early representations of the Torah-shrine, such as those on the mosaic floor of the synagogue from Beth Shean, used classical rather than twisted columns. When the Baroque style became less fashionable, the use of twisted columns diminished but did not disappear. They can be seen in many nineteenth-century synagogues.

THE DECALOGUE

The rounded tablets of stone, the decalogue, also have an interesting history as Jewish symbols. In 1215 the Lateran Council under Pope Innocent III introduced badges for Jews in order to discourage social relations between Christians and Jews. The

Fig. 17 *Torah mantle; green velvet with a central panel of French silk. Relief embroidery in gold thread. Bohemia, Bydzor, 1743. (State Jewish Museum, Prague; photo: Whitworth Art Gallery. Manchester.)*

diagram 5 *The decalogue.*

English Jewish badge consisted of the rounded tablets of the Law so familiar to us today. This particular form did not appear as a representation of the decalogue until medieval times, when the tablets were used upon cathedrals with figures representing Judaism defeated as opposed to Christianity triumphant. The tablets were portrayed variously as square, rectangular or in book form before the now familiar rounded shape became generally accepted.

In Jewish symbolism the rounded tablets appeared first in manuscripts, and were not used in ritual art before the fifteenth or early sixteenth centuries. The El Transito Synagogue of Toledo, 1357, has two arch-shaped windows placed centrally in the eastern wall over the position where the Ark would have stood, but the first representation of the tablets of stone over the Ark as we know it today is probably that in the Portuguese synagogue in Holland (1671–5).

Lions rampant each side of the decalogue

The symbol of two lions rampant each side of the decalogue is almost certainly a Baroque development. Lions have been used since antiquity to flank the Ark, but not necessarily rampant. Thus this symbol, used so unceasingly upon all conventional Torah mantles and many Ark curtains today, has a pedigree of only 300 years – not very long by Jewish standards!

ק״ק שערי צדק

diagram 6 *A fine interpretation of the lions rampant each side of the decalogue by Fred Kormis for the North Western Reform Synagogue, London. They appear on the Ark doors and are used as a logo.*

ANIMALS

Animal ornamentation is far more ancient. Lions were favoured in ancient synagogue frescoes from the Romanesque and Gothic periods. The lion symbolizes the tribe of Judah, but it also represents strength and justice.

The peacock can be found from ancient times as a symbol of immortality and the Messianic Age.

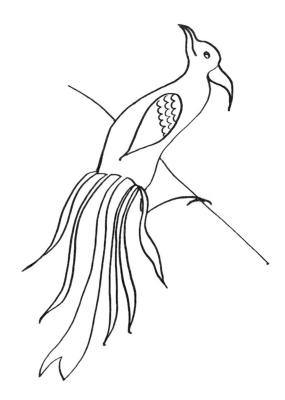

diagram 7 *Embroidered peacock from a tallit in the Israel Museum.*

The Behemoth and Leviathan, a fantastic beast and a giant fish respectively, represent legendary creatures upon whom the righteous are supposed to feast at the end of days. They can be seen on ancient synagogue mosaics as well as in illuminated manuscripts and antique prayer books.

The four animals as the four qualities of the pious Jew

Earlier I described the cherubim as composite creatures made up from four different animals (page 00). Rachel Wischnitzer has traced the development of these mythical creatures from Ezekiel's vision to the four qualities of the pious Jew as written in the *Sayings of the Fathers*:

> Be as strong as a lion
> As swift as the eagle
> Fleet as the deer and
> Bold as the leopard to do
> The will of your Father in Heaven

The four animals symbolized the virtues of the pious Jew in a manuscript in the Vatican dated

Fig. 19 *Parokhet of many fabrics, with symbolism including the Tree of Life and the four animals which symbolize the attributes of the pious Jew. (Jenny Glaser for the Leo Baeck Centre, East Kew, Victoria, Australia.)*

Fig. 18 *The doors of the Holy Ark of the Wolff Popper Butzian Synagogue, Cracow. Carved and painted wood, Cracow, seventeenth century. (Museum of the Chief Rabbinate, Hechal Schlomo, Jerusalem.)*

1436 and were very popular in eighteenth- and nineteenth-century folk art. They were carved on the Ark and on the bimah in Poland, printed on the flags which children carried on Simchat Torah (Rejoicing of the Law), and embroidered upon Torah binders. Examples of folk art from this period are charming and could well provide inspiration for contemporary embroiderers.

THE TREE OF LIFE

The Tree of Life is a common symbol in many religions. It originated as a fertility symbol in Mesopotamia in the region of the Tigris and the Euphrates about 2,850 BCE. One thousand years later it was portrayed as a date palm. The vine and the olive tree have also been used to depict the Tree of Life. The twisted pillars used so much in Baroque

Fig. 20 *The Tree of Life, detail of a Torah mantle* (colour plate 1), *by Kathryn Salomon, for the North Western Reform Synagogue, London.*

Fig. 21 *Embroidery for Elijah's chair (used to hold the baby during the circumcision ceremony) by Deborah Kelman, Oakland, California. Cotton velveteen, batiked and embroidered.*

synagogue decoration sometimes had grape-vines entwined around them.

For Jews the Tree of Life is a symbol of the Messianic Age, of the Day of Judgement and of life after death. It is also associated in Jewish tradition with mystical Judaism, the cabbalah, and with the Torah itself. The wooden staves at each end of the Torah scroll are known as 'Trees of Life' (Etzei Hayim). During the Torah service we refer to the Torah as 'A Tree of Life to those who grasp it'.

The following description of the Tree of Life from Daniel 4 v8–10 would be exciting portrayed in any medium,

And behold a tree in the midst of the earth,
And the height thereof was great.

41

The tree grew and was strong,
And the height thereof reached unto the
  heaven,
And the sight thereof to the end of the earth.
The leaves thereof were fair, and the fruit
  thereof much,
And in it was food for all,
The beasts of the field had shadow under it,
And the fowls of the heaven dwelt in the
  branches thereof,
And all flesh was fed of it.

THE FLAME

The flame can represent the 'ner tamid', the light which burns continuously in front of the Ark in the synagogue as a symbol of God's presence, or the Burning Bush. Since the Holocaust it has also taken on associations with that dark period in Jewish history.

Fig. 22 *Israeli stamp with a flame design which incorporates the words 'Shema Israel' (Hear O Israel).*

Fig. 23 *Detail of a parokhet of velvet with machine embroidery which uses the same design. (Stanmore Synagogue, Middlesex.)*

It is interesting to follow the development of symbolism. We know that the invention of printing had a great influence upon design. Early printers often used the same prints for different books for economic reasons, and Jews were frequently forbidden from possessing printing presses and had their books printed by Gentiles. Rachel Wischnitzer has described how the Holbein Lyon Bible of 1538

Fig. 24 High Holy Day Torah mantle; gold thread and silk organza appliqué. Designed by Edward Toledano and embroidered by Estelle Levy for the Spanish and Portuguese Jews Congregation, London. One of a pair.

and the Mantua *Haggadah* of 1560 share common illustrations, although they have different captions. (Jews learnt of the work of Michelangelo, Holbein and Raphael in this way.) It was common practice for both Jewish and Gentile craftsmen to copy well-known artists' work on to faience dishes and other items. This process still continues today. I have long felt that the flame design which has become popular in British synagogues came about because of the Holocaust. When I spoke about this to Rabbi Chaitowitz of Stanmore Synagogue, he told me about an Israeli stamp with the flame made out of the words 'Shema Israel' ('Hear O Israel') in just the way the flame upon so many embroideries had been designed. A philatelist found the stamp for me; it was issued by the Israeli Government in 1962 as part of a set of two stamps to commemorate the heroes of the Holocaust and was designed by Mrs Mersusy and Mrs Ornan.

THE TWELVE TRIBES

The Twelve Tribes of Israel are often used and can be striking and effective. Although some have definite emblems and colours, others have been portrayed with different symbols and colours by some artists.

Tribe	Colour	Symbol
Reuben	Red	Mandrakes (Gen. 30:14)
Simeon	Green	Town of Shechem (Gen. 34:25)
Levi	White/black/red	Urim and Thummin (Deut. 33:8) (The Urim and Thummin were bundles of sticks or bones used by the Priests for obtaining oracles)
Judah	Azure	Lion (Gen. 49:9)
Issachar	Black	Strong-boned ass (Gen. 49:14)
Zebulun	White	A ship (Gen. 49:13)
Dan	Sapphire	Serpent (Gen. 49:17) or Lion's whelp (Deut. 33:22)
Gad	Grey	Tent (Gen. 49:19) or Lion (Deut. 33:20)
Naphtali	Rose	Hind (Gen. 49:21)
Ephraim and Menassah		Black bullock and wild ox (Deut. 33:17)
Benjamin	12 colours	Wolf (Gen. 49:27)

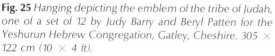

Fig. 25 Hanging depicting the emblem of the tribe of Judah, one of a set of 12 by Judy Barry and Beryl Patten for the Yeshurun Hebrew Congregation, Gatley, Cheshire. 305 × 122 cm (10 × 4 ft).

Fig. 26 Hanging: 'Homage to the Ten Lost Tribes', Rebecca Consiver. (Mount Vernon, New York.)

Fig. 27 High Holy Day Torah mantle; oyster-coloured satin with d'Alençon lace, designed by Rabbi Reinhart and embroidered by Beryl Dean MBE. (Westminster Synagogue, London.)

Fig. 28 *Ark doors for the High Holy Days by Naomi Cohen-Ziv. A variety of fabrics with machine and hand embroidery, trapunto quilting, beads and cords. The crown measures 150 cm² (4 ft 11 in.) square. (North Western Reform Synagogue, London.)*

WATER

The Tree of Life, the flame and water are universal symbols which everyone can understand and which can be applied very dramatically in Judaic embroidery. Water is a very powerful metaphor for life whether it is the theme of 'Living Water' from the Psalms or the parting of the Red Sea. It can be very successfully adapted for abstract design.

THE CROWN

The crown can often be seen upon parochot or Torah mantles. Sometimes three crowns are shown: the crown of the priesthood, the crown of the Law, and the crown of the monarchy.

THE STAR OF DAVID

The symbol most commonly associated with Judaism today is the six-pointed star. Its 'Jewish' pedigree is very tenuous and its adoption comparatively recent.

The six-pointed star has been used since the Bronze Age by many civilizations from Mesopotamia to Britain for magical purposes and in alchemy. It can

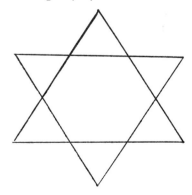

diagram 8 *The Star of David.*

be seen on ancient papyri in the British Museum and on amulets from the Cairo Geniza. The oldest undisputed use of the star amongst Jews dates from 7 BCE in Sidon, where it was used on the seal of Joshua ben Asayahu.

At the time of Herod's Temple it was used by Jews and non-Jews. Christians, Jews and Muslims all used it in the Middle Ages. In 1354 King Charles IV granted the Prague Jewish community the privilege of its own flag which contained the six-pointed star and it is possible that this helped to promote it as a Jewish emblem.

The earliest use in a synagogue is probably in the seventeenth century in Bavaria, where the synagogue at Furth had circular windows incorporating the star.

There is a theory that the Star of David became popular when the Jews, emerging from the ghettos in the seventeenth and eighteenth centuries, wanted a symbol in the way the Christians have a central symbol in the cross. It did not become really popular until the nineteenth century. In the present century the Nazis forced all Jews in the countries they occupied to wear the Magen David to differentiate them, just as Jews were marked out in the past. After the birth of the State of Israel it was incorporated into the Israeli flag. The badge of shame became the badge of pride.

PLANTS

The plants associated with the land of Israel can and have been used symbolically in many media.

Pomegranates
These are mentioned in Exodus 28 as being embroidered upon the priestly robes. They also represent fertility.

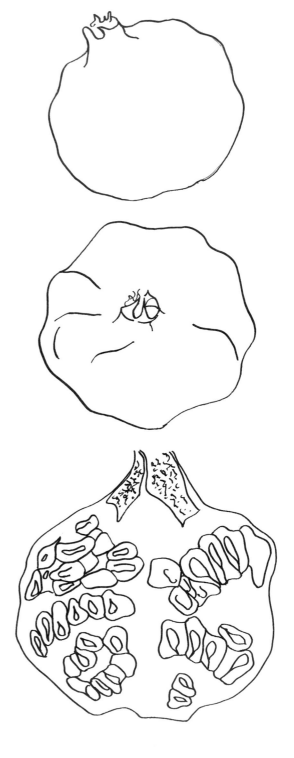

diagrams 9, 10, 11 *A pomegranate.*

Fig. 29 *'And you shall take of the fruits of the land', by Francine Fierstein and Sylvia Wolff. It depicts the seven species and was commissioned by the Director of Education, the New York Botanical Garden. Felt appliqué and embroidery, 53 cm (21 in.) in diameter.*

The seven species
Deuteronomy 8:8 names seven species with which the land of Israel is blessed. They are barley, figs, honey, olives, pomegranates, wheat and the vine.

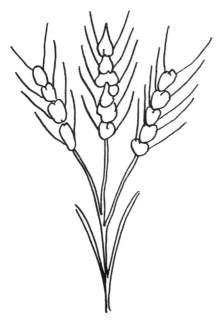

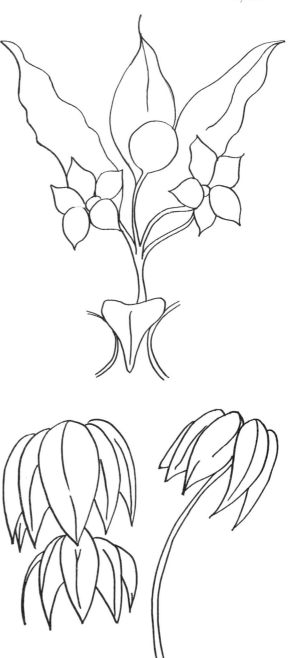

diagrams 12, 13, 14 *'Fruits of the Holy Land' from the capitals of pillars of the Brighton and Hove Hebrew Congregation Synagogue.*

diagram 15 *The vine.*

The vine

The vine has already been mentioned as a symbol of the Tree of Life, and as one of the seven species. It has other meanings too. The children of Israel are referred to as a vine in Isaiah 5:7 and Hosea 9:10. The vine has been used to represent Jerusalem and the Torah (*Hullin* 92a), and also, of course, it symbolizes wine.

A magnificent golden vine hung over the inner portal of the Second Temple. People would donate single golden grapes or bunches of grapes which were added to the vine. There is a well-known carving of a grape-vine carved in the space above the lintel in the Altneu Synagogue at Prague.

JERUSALEM

The holy city itself has been used in ceremonial art over the ages. Often it is shown in a circular space at the centre of a design which recalls ancient maps with Jerusalem at the centre of the world. This goes back to an even more ancient prototype where Babylon is shown in the centre of a map of the world.

Fig. 30 *Canvas work panel of Jerusalem by Bonni Yales, Lexington, Massachusetts.*

THE WAILING WALL

This last remnant of the Temple has been an emotive symbol for Jews throughout the ages. In fact, it is not part of the actual Temple, but a fragment of the outer western wall. However, the wall draws a deep

Fig. 31 *Detail of Torah mantle by Bonni Yales, Closter, New York.*

THE HIGH HOLY DAYS
(THE NEW YEAR, TEN DAYS OF PENITENCE AND THE DAY OF ATONEMENT)

White is used at these times to symbolize purity and a fresh start to the New Year. Although bleaching

Fig. 32 *Parokhet for the High Holy Days, nineteenth century. Metal thread embroidery, spangles and jewels. (Property of a Yeshiva in London.)*

emotional response from all who visit it and has been depicted in so many commercial prints, drawings, embroidery kits and so forth that it is difficult to bring a fresh approach to the subject. Matty Grunberg, an Israeli artist, has produced a piece which does look at the wall in a new way and which may give the embroiderer food for thought. He has exploited the hugeness of the slabs of stone, and the crevices and gaps between them. The general irregularity of the surface due to the erosion and pitting of the stonework has also been explored by him. A semi-abstract design making use of the textures and layers of the wall could be a starting point for some original contemporary designs.

To these general symbols one can add specific ones for the Sabbath or for special festivals.

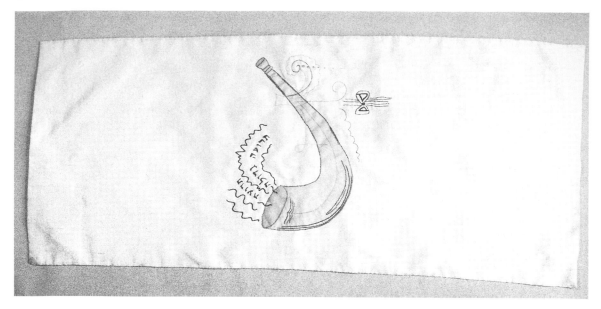

Fig. 33 *Bag for a shofar; appliqué organza embroidered with silk threads, by Esther Carvalho, London.*

was known to the ancient Egyptians who left cotton in the sun, a brilliant white, such as we use today, was unobtainable before the invention of synthetic bleach by Charles Tennant in 1799. This means that until the nineteenth century the colour white would not have been white at all, but a soft, natural cream. Perhaps we should think again about the High Holy Day fabrics. The soft, creamy colour used by our ancestors is far more pleasing aesthetically.

The shofar or ram's horn is the symbol associated with this period as it is blown on the New Year and the Day of Atonement.

In the home, apple is dipped into honey and eaten to symbolize a sweet New Year. This could make a pleasant symbol for domestic embroidery, but is less suitable for the synagogue.

SUCCOT (FEAST OF TABERNACLES)

The harvest festival of Succot is celebrated by building a hut or booth and decorating it with fruit and flowers. Families eat their meals in the Succah,

Fig. 34 *High Holy Day Torah Mantle depicting the lulav and the etrog; appliqué of man-made suede with top stitching. The etrog is made of canvas work and appliquéd to the ground fabric. (Leni Taussig, Maine Island, British Columbia.)*

and some live in it for the full week of the festival. The lulav, literally 'palm branch', but used to describe a bundle of willow, palm and myrtle, and the etrog, a fruit which resembles a lemon, are held and shaken symbolically during the synagogue service. Illustrations of the lulav and etrog have been used in synagogue art and on ceremonial objects since antiquity. Harvest fruits can also be used for domestic items.

PESACH (PASSOVER)

Passover is celebrated in the spring, so all the symbols of spring and renewed life are appropriate.

A dish is placed upon the table at the Passover service in the home, which is known as the Seder, containing various items which are either eaten or

Fig. 35 *Passover cloth by Ella Schwab, Germany; turn of the century. The cloth illustrates the four sons referred to in the Seder service as representations of the four types of Jew. (Property of Mr Simons.)*

referred to symbolically. The Seder dish, with its various symbolic foods, can be used for decoration on items used during the Seder service (such as the matzah cloth). The components of the Seder dish are as follows: bitter herbs, usually horseradish and parsley, a bone to represent the Pascal lamb (a lamb can be used as a symbol instead of a bone), a mixture of nuts, wine, raisins, apple and cinnamon called haroseth which represents the mortar the Israelites had to make when they built the pyramids. (This mixture is difficult to portray pictorially and is often represented by a wheelbarrow, being the container used for transporting building materials. Sometimes dishes for the haroseth are made in the shape of a wheelbarrow.) The Temple offering is represented by a roasted egg. Matzah, unleavened bread, is eaten during the eight days of Passover, and can be used as decoration for a matzah cloth (see *fig. 105*).

During the Seder service four types of Jews are represented in a passage about four sons – one wise,

one wicked, one simple and one who is too young to question. They have been used to make effective decorative symbols for Passover embroideries.

SHAVUOT (PENTECOST)

The Season of the Giving of the Law, Shavuot, comes in early summer. During this festival the book of Ruth is read because it is the time of the barley harvest in Israel. The synagogue is decorated with flowers for the festival, and in the past some synagogues used a special green parokhet. Although there is no specific symbolism for Shavuot, flowers, barley and the colour green are appropriate.

In Polish communities, in earlier times, the windows of the houses were decorated with

Fig. 37 *Detail of* fig. 36.

Fig. 38 *Papercut mizrach by Yehudit Shadur, Jerusalem.*

papercuts for Shavuot. This theme can be used as an inspiration for a Shavuot parokhet with the design worked out as a papercut, or based on a papercut design, thus recalling the folk tradition of a bygone age.

SHABBAT (SABBATH)

See challah cloths (page 129).

COLOUR SYMBOLISM

There is only one colour which must be used symbolically at a specific time of the year in Jewish tradition – this is white, which is used for the New Year, the Ten Days of Penitence and the Day of Atonement (see page 49).

Green is sometimes used for Shavuot, and in the

Fig. 36 *Parokhet with a floral design in silk embroidery by Isaac Sassoon, London.*

past black was used for the 9th Av, a fast in remembrance of the destruction of the Temple.

One or two modern synagogues use different vestments for different times of the year, or for the Pilgrim or Foot Festivals (the festivals of Succot, Pesach and Shavuot, when the people used to take offerings of the first fruits to the Temple).

Red, blue, purple and 'linen' are referred to in Exodus 25–8 as colours which were used in the desert Sanctuary. According to Josephus, they were used in the second Temple and he gives elaborate symbolic reasons for their use. Red, blue and purple have always been royal colours used by monarchies and priesthoods. Linen may be seen as the undyed, natural colour, perhaps symbolic of earth, but also perhaps simply as the ancient equivalent of white.

This varied list shows just how rich the symbolism used for Jewish embroidery can be. So often in synagogues in Britain today one sees the same motifs repeated again and again: usually the lions rampant each side of the tablets of stone, topped by the Magen David. There is no excuse for this lack of imagination; let us hope that we shall see a greater variety of symbols used in the future.

chapter four

Design

As so many Jewish religious ceremonies take place in the home there are many embroideries which can be made for personal or domestic use.

When items are made for individuals, either for oneself or as a commission, there can be complete freedom in the choice of colour, material and design. The personal whims and fancies of the patron can be fully satisfied. However, when one designs an object for a public building such as a synagogue, there are various criteria which must be borne in mind. The design must be sympathetic to the architectural surroundings for which it is intended. Colours and materials should blend harmoniously with their surroundings. Synagogues may commission work directly from the artist, and designs will then be submitted to a committee who will have to approve them. Sometimes a patron will approach an artist and commission a vestment without consulting the synagogue, or it may happen that a craftsperson will make and donate an item personally. There is no point in a patron or an artist being offended if he or she donates something which the synagogue does not use frequently because it is unsuitable. Even though a privately commissioned vestment does not have to be shown to a committee, the same criteria apply. A very modern piece can harmonize well with more traditional elements, but not always. If every other Torah mantle is made of dark blue velvet, one in a bright furnishing fabric will stick out like a sore thumb.

DESIGN METHODS

No one should be afraid of designing. The average person who arranges furniture in the home, cooks a meal with an eye to its colour and appearance as well as taste, or arranges flowers, knows more about design than she or he realizes.

Fig. 39 *Seed head used in the design for the large desk cover for the North Western Reform Synagogue, London (colour plate 6). The seed head was drawn and photographed, as were many other plants.*

Ideas rarely come into one's mind without any effort at all. It is a good idea to have a notebook in which to jot down ideas as they occur, to be referred to at a later date. Collecting postcards or photographs of things one finds particularly appealing can also prove useful. This is for reference, *not* copying purposes. No one should copy someone else's design or reproduce an old item. Illuminated manuscripts and folk art from the Jewish past can prove to be starting points for interesting compositions. Quotations from the Bible can spark off an exciting idea and so help to avoid the clichés which can dominate religious work.

Having settled upon an idea, play around with it for a while. Experiment in pencil and in colour, or perhaps with cut-paper shapes. Sketching from nature, both in pencil and in watercolour, is both satisfying and helpful for design purposes.

A good method of improving an original idea is to draw it upon greaseproof paper pinned to a drawing board. You can then lay a fresh piece of greaseproof paper over the sketch and redraw the areas you wish to include and omit the areas to be changed. (The process is much easier if a lightbox is available.)

When the line drawing is completed, it should be translated into colour. It is worth spending a reasonable length of time at the drawing board, working out as many of the design problems as possible. All ambiguities will have to be cleared up at some point, and exact lines and colours will have to be chosen, and it is preferable to do this sooner rather than later. It is important to work out the design in colour at this stage so that tone and mass can be judged and balanced. When a design has been decided upon, it should be enlarged to full size as scale can change both shape and proportions. Many people use a grid to enlarge a design, but the method shown in diagrams 16 and 17 works accurately for all shapes and sizes of designs, even if they are not exact. The design can be enlarged very accurately by this method.

It is not necessary to start from drawings when designing. Cut paper can be placed upon a background and arranged to give a pleasing effect. Papercuts are a traditional Jewish art and can be

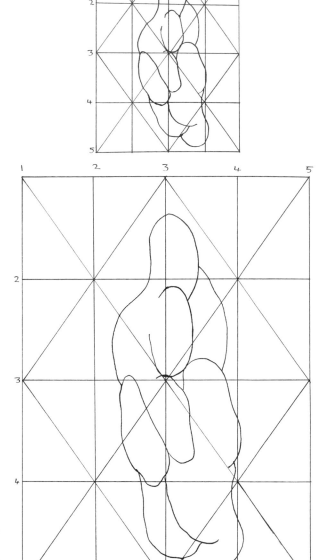

diagrams 16, 17 *Enlarging a design by means of ruling diagonal lines across it. There is no need to take measurements. First make a diagonal cross between the corners, then quarter the page. All the centre points will meet. The design can be subdivided by this method to make each section as small as is desirable. The horizontal and vertical lines are then numbered to make it easier to locate and transpose different features.*

Fig. 40 *Papercut by Yehudit Shadur, Jerusalem.*

Fig. 41 *Parokhet by Yael Shiloh, Israel. Patchwork with appliqué and embroidery.*

used to produce a modern design. Yehudit Shadur is a modern papercut artist who works in Israel and who has designed embroideries for the synagogue based on the papercut technique.

The Hebrew alphabet is very beautiful and can be manipulated to produce striking compositions. Hebrew lettering is so important that a complete chapter has been devoted to it (pages 141–51).

WORKING ON A DESIGN

When working on a piece of embroidery, care should be taken not to start in one corner and gradually work one's way to the opposite side. Ideas can change as the work develops and if areas are completely finished the design cannot evolve. It is far better to 'dot around' the work, choosing different areas and never completing any one place for as long as possible. This helps one achieve a fluid, unified composition. The embroiderer's style must inevitably develop and change during the course of any project, and one needs to avoid working in such a way that the observer can see where the embroidery has been started and where it has been finished.

chapter five

Embroidery materials and techniques

BACKGROUND FABRICS

Ceremonial items for the synagogue receive very hard wear and must be made of durable fabrics. Obviously one would always make the parokhet of a furnishing fabric, but it is possible that the embroiderer would not consider this necessary for a Torah mantle. The mantles can receive very rough treatment and a furnishing fabric is needed here too. Many synagogues in Britain use velvet for their parochot and Torah mantles. This is only custom, and specifically an Ashkenazi custom.

No final choice of fabric for any item for the synagogue should be made without seeing the material at the synagogue both in daylight and by electric light. Synagogues are used in the evening as well as in the day, and materials can change their colour in different lights. The fabrics need to harmonize with the architectural features and existing items in the synagogue. It is important to stand well back when assessing a fabric sample in relation to its intended surroundings. This is the only way to gain a true impression.

One must also consider how well the fabric stands up to strong sunlight. Some fabrics, silk for instance, perish in sunlight and if an embroidery is to be hung in a position which catches the sun for any length of time, this must be borne in mind.

The best materials possible should always be purchased. Items for a synagogue should last a long

time, and it is worth remembering the time expended on the embroidery is the same whether inferior or superior materials are used. Articles last much longer if good-quality fabrics and other materials are employed.

If the embroiderer intends to use metal-thread embroidery, a material with a close weave such as silk or satin will have to be used as a background fabric. (The reverse side of satin can be used if a shiny surface is not required.) Velvet is a very popular fabric for synagogue use, but it is very difficult to work. It cannot be rolled on to a frame and all the embroidered areas need to be worked over a backing such as felt, because of the velvet pile. It marks very easily, so the embroider cannot radically change the design once it has been transferred to the velvet. Great care has to be taken when tacking or using pins, as these too can leave marks.

Felt can be applied to any area which is to be embroidered. The embroiderer can then work directly upon the design. Pale yellow felt is used beneath goldwork and white or grey beneath silver. Silk can be appliquéd to other areas or motifs can be worked on calico and then appliquéd to the velvet.

It is possible to work lettering on velvet in the following manner: a piece of canvas which has not been locked or heavily glued, and from which threads can easily be removed, such as waste canvas, is laid over the velvet, and secured by a suitable means. The lettering is then worked in

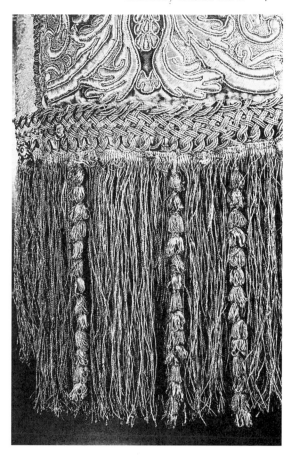

Figs. 42, 43 *Detail of metal thread embroidery from a Torah mantle; early eighteenth century, Spanish and Portuguese Jews Congregation, London (See fig. 65 for the complete mantle.)*

canvas-work techniques and afterwards the canvas threads are pulled away. It will be necessary to experiment to be sure that the stitches will not be too loose once the canvas has been removed.

Gold fabric is best avoided if the embroiderer intends to use metal-thread embroidery, as the threads will not stand out against the background. I used a gold-coloured silk as the background for some desk covers because I wanted the colour of the background material to blend with the colour of the bimah area as a whole. It was necessary to raise the metal threads and to use appliqué and stitchery to set off the goldwork.

Fabrics which crease easily are unsuitable for Torah mantles, as are delicate materials which are

likely to catch and snag on the Torah ornaments. Practicality must also be considered when choosing embroidery techniques. Long lengths of purl, gold plate, and long loose threads are not suitable.

It is a good idea to keep samples of materials and threads used for any particular project in a file with all their particulars. This enables the embroiderer to locate and order any item speedily and easily. The file will become a useful source of reference at a later date when the embroidery is no longer to hand.

THREADS

The wide range of threads available for secular embroidery are all suitable for Jewish ceremonial work. Metal-thread embroidery which has always

59

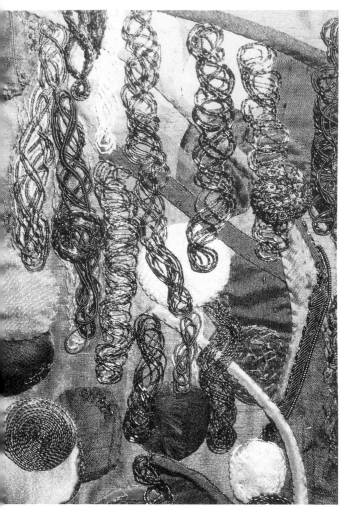

Fig. 44 *Detail of the large desk cover (jacket illustration), North Western Reform Synagogue, London, showing a variety of couched metal threads and purls.*

been used for religious vestments, both ecclesiastical and Jewish ceremonial, is of course particularly suitable for the synagogue, as it makes a rich and dramatic effect from a distance. Goldwork is time-consuming and costly and the embroiderer needs to learn special techniques.

Admiralty quality – the best-quality gold threads – should always be used as they tarnish less readily than cheaper varieties. Artificial gold threads should be treated with caution; they can be used to supplement the more expensive threads, but can look cheap and tawdry if not used with care. Leathers and kids, in silver, gold and other colours, can enrich a design. Here again, care is needed. They are expensive but can look cheap if used too freely.

Metal threads

Metal threads can be obtained in both gold and silver, although silver has a tendency to tarnish more quickly than gold, and can turn black. 'Antique' gold and silver, mixed with a small amount of black, are available in some types. Copper threads can be obtained, as can aluminium. The latter is less attractive than silver. Most of the threads listed below are available in a number of thicknesses:

Jap gold
As its name implies, it comes from Japan. Real Jap gold is no longer available and a substitute (which does not tarnish) is now used. Jap consists of a flat metal which has been cut into strips and wound around a silk core.

Passing
A gold thread is wound around a core.

Rococo or check
This thread has a kink in it and can be an interesting contrast in texture.

Purls

A continuous spring of metal manufactured in a number of finishes. It is cut in varying lengths and used in many ways to achieve rich and surprisingly varied effects. Rough or wire purl has a dull appearance, and smooth is brighter. Check is constructed so that it sparkles and pearl purl is far more rigid. The latter is gently pulled out before being applied.

Twists and cords
Different thickness and textures are available and can be combined to give a rich effect.

Spangles and beads
Spangles are not to be confused with sequins. They have a more subtle appearance. Beads should be used with caution. Sometimes the embroiderer can find old braids and sequins at an antique market.

Fancy metal threads
Brightly coloured synthetic and metal threads, dark lurex threads and copper threads, are all obtainable. They can be blended with the more expensive materials to give a rich and exciting design, but need to be treated with care so that a tawdry effect is not produced.

Working with metal threads
Metal thread embroidery must be worked on a square frame with a strong calico backing, as both hands must be free. (Details on framing up are given on page 00.)

Great care has to be taken when working with metal threads. They must be stored wrapped in acid-free tissue paper away from the damp or they will tarnish. The embroiderer should always make sure her hands are clean when working upon any embroidery, but extra care needs to be taken when using metal threads. Hot or damp, sticky hands can make the threads tarnish more quickly. As much of the embroidery as possible should be covered when work is in progress to keep off dust and sunlight. It should always be covered when the embroiderer is not working upon it. A clean towel should be placed on the areas of the frame upon which the embroiderer's arms rest whilst she is working, to protect that area and keep it clean.

Various methods of working metal threads will be discussed here briefly. Anyone considering using this type of embroidery should produce a sampler, experiment with different ways of using the threads, and consult a number of books on the subject. *A Dictionary of Metal Thread Embroidery* by Jane Lemon, *Metal Thread Embroidery* by Barbara Dawson and *Embroidery in Religion and Ceremonial* by Beryl Dean are all especially useful.

Metal threads are usually couched down two threads at a time. The threads are left on the surface whilst an area is worked, and only then taken through to the back with a chenille needle or with a loop of thread.

Threads can be couched with different-coloured silks to change the colour of the gold (or silver). A fine silk called Maltese silk used to be available for couching down metal threads, but it is unobtainable now, and a strong sewing silk or cotton in a suitable colour is used instead. All threads for couching are passed through a piece of beeswax to strengthen them.

String can be laid down either regularly, or in a random fashion to alter and vary the surface of the goldwork. It should be dyed with coffee or tea to ensure that any small amount which might peep through is unobtrusive.

Purls are cut on a velvet tray before they are used. The embroiderer should experiment with laying them down in different ways as they are very versatile. They should be handled with tweezers whenever possible. Purls have a tendency to tarnish faster than some other metal threads. It is a good idea to use an untarnishable thread next to an area of purl so that the essential line of the design can be seen even if the purls have tarnished. The embroiderer should not be too discouraged by the thought of the threads tarnishing. This is part of the beauty of real gold as opposed to artificial gold threads. They mellow and change. Areas can be manipulated to achieve different colours of gold and add richness and life to the embroidery.

Goldwork can be raised in just the same way as appliqué by the use of padding with felt. The designated shape is cut out in felt – pale yellow for gold, white or grey for silver. Several pieces of felt, all the same shape, are cut in decreasing sizes. The number depends on the amount the embroiderer wishes to raise the area. The smallest piece of felt is sewn to the background fabric first and then the pieces are sewn one on top of the other in ascending sizes until the area has been built up. Raised work has been used traditionally for Jewish ceremonial embroidery. Antique parochot and Torah mantles can be seen with rich, plastic areas worked in gold and silver.

Fig. 45 *Detail of the large desk cover (jacket illustration), North Western Reform Synagogue, London, showing purls laid over a cord to form a raised stem. Pearl purl can be seen laid over the raised stem and also couched over Jap gold. The flower bud in the centre is raised Jap gold.*

It is a good idea to make a sampler of the material to be used for the embroidery. Ideas can be freely explored and different techniques tried without working and unpicking the actual embroidery.

Sometimes when working an area one becomes dissatisfied with a particular part. It is best to leave it rather than unpick it immediately. (Unpicking is not a good idea – it weakens the background fabric.) If another area is worked and the problem area returned to at a later date, it may be found that a simple solution comes to mind, or that the problem has disappeared when the embroidery is viewed as a whole.

Whilst working on a design, one should look at it from a distance every so often. An embroiderer should always stand well back to assess a design, but this is particularly important in the case of work for a public building such as a synagogue. One becomes so used to seeing embroidery at close quarters that it is easy to forget that most people will view it from a distance.

EQUIPMENT

Design equipment
Pencils
Paper
Eraser
Drawing board
Watercolours or gouache paint
A selection of coloured papers if designing with cut
   paper rather than paint
Ruler
Greaseproof or tracing paper
Scissors to be kept especially for cutting paper

Equipment for transferring the design

A pricker (a needle fixed into some kind of holder or cork)

Pounce (a mixture of talcum powder or ground cuttlefish, and charcoal. The two substances are mixed to make a suitable colour for the background fabric – lighter for a dark fabric, and darker for a light fabric)

Different coloured threads for tacking different lines

A fine sable paint brush with a good point

Watercolour paint

Sewing materials

A frame

Pins

Cotton, silk and fancy threads

Three pairs of scissors: one for cutting out the background fabric, one pair for general use and a small pair which is kept especially for cutting metal threads.

A melor (an implement with a flat and a pointed end for manipulating gold threads)

Tweezers

Beeswax for use with metal threads

A range of needles, sharps for general sewing purposes and some metal threadwork

Crewel needles for embroidering with cotton and silks

Chenille needles for pulling through metal threads

A packing needle for framing up

Tacking cotton

Acid-free tissue paper

String, both for framing up and to produce texture

Strong synthetic thread for framing up

TRANSFERRING THE DESIGN TO THE BACKGROUND FABRIC

The traditional method for transferring designs is to trace the design on to tracing paper. A needle is fitted into a holder (if one is not available, try a piece of cork or some other substitute). Place the tracing paper on a piece of folded felt and then carefully prick the lines of the design.

The design can be transferred either before or after the material has been framed up.

diagram 18 *Pricking the design.*

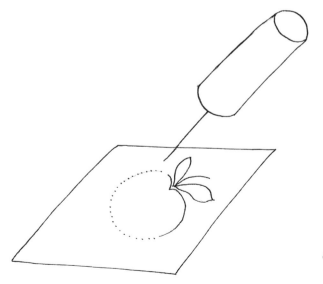

diagram 19 *Applying the pounce.*

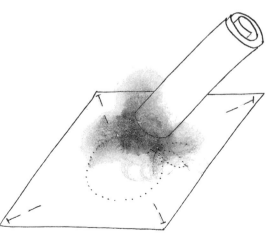

Advantages of transferring the design after the material has been framed up

Whenever possible the design should be transferred after the material has been framed. The material is held secure and flat and it is simple to align the horizontal, vertical and centre lines of the design and the fabric.

Reasons for transferring the design before the material has been framed

When a design is so large that the material cannot be attached to the frame with the complete design on the frame, the design has to be transferred before framing up. Make sure that the material is completely flat and that it is held down with weights.

Transferring the design

The pounce is rubbed on to the tracing (which has been carefully fixed to the material) with small circular movements. Take care to work in one direction and do not go back over areas previously worked. Remove the tracing with care and paint in the lines of the design over the marks left by the pounce. Blow or flick away surplus pounce.

Tacking a design to the background fabric

The design is traced on to greaseproof paper or tissue paper and pinned to the fabric. The main lines are tacked and the paper is then ripped away leaving the tacked design. If different coloured threads are used for different lines, the design will be clearer. This is the method used for velvet when pricking and pouncing is not suitable.

Other methods of transferring a design

There are special pens on the market which can be used to transfer a design or draw straight on to the fabric. First check that they are suitable on a small test area. A design can also be painted directly on to the fabric. Pencil is best avoided as it makes the embroidery threads dirty. The embroiderer should treat with caution any method which leaves a permanent mark upon the background fabric. For this reason it is best to paint only the main lines of a design and to tack minor lines so that the design can be changed and developed.

Transparent fabrics

The design is placed beneath the fabric and the two elements fixed on to a light-box or an improvised light-box. The design can then be transferred directly on to the fabric.

FRAMING UP

A frame is used for ceremonial embroidery for a number of reasons:

1 It prevents puckering of the material during work on the embroidery.

2 The fabric is kept in a fresher condition during the work and needs little attention or pressing afterwards.

3 The design can be seen as a whole and can be developed with ease.

It may take longer to produce a piece of work on a frame but superior results are obtained.

Types of frame

Circular or tambour frames

These are available in different sizes with or without stands. They are not as satisfactory as a square frame as the material tends to slip and become slack. Small areas can be worked on a tambour frame and applied later to the background fabric.

Square or slate frames

These are available in a variety of sizes. Tapestry frames can be bought with stands. The frame is supported upon a trestle or by some other method, perhaps against a chair or between two tables.

Small square or rectangular frames can be made by fixing four pieces of wood together, making sure that the corners are at right-angles. It may be necessary to put a metal right-angle over the corners of a slightly larger frame.

Dressing the frame

Unbleached calico is applied to the frame as a backing. It must be washed before use as it will shrink. When it has been ironed the calico is cut to size and the centre marked. Care must be taken to cut on the straight of grain, with the selvedge running the length of the embroidery. A piece of string is folded into the sides of the calico and machined into position. This strengthens the sides. The centre line of the calico is marked and pinned to the centre point of the webbing. The calico can be turned to give a small hem if necessary. Starting from the centre point, the calico is stitched to the webbing with a straight stitch. The process is repeated in the opposite direction. Care must be taken to apply the material straight.

The side pieces of the frame are inserted and the pegs placed so that the material is reasonably taut.

A large-eyed strong needle, such as a packing needle, is used to lace the string to the sides of the frame. The string is laced through the backing and over the sides of the frame and secured at each end. It is now possible to pull the string so that the backing is firm.

Applying the background fabric to the backing
The background fabric is cut on the straight of grain, with the selvedge running the length of the embroidery. A large margin is left around the design. This is important as the design can then expand if necessary as work progresses. The centre line of the fabric is marked with a line of tacking and matched up to the line of the backing material. The fabric is always attached to a slack frame; it is carefully pinned on to the backing with the pins pointing

diagram 20 *The dressed frame.*

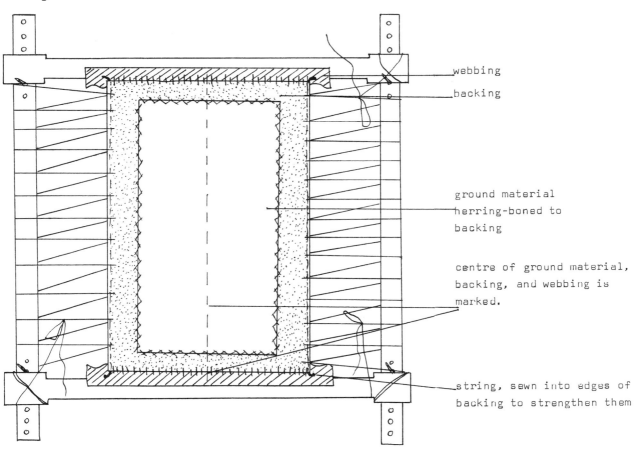

webbing

backing

ground material herring-boned to backing

centre of ground material, backing, and webbing is marked.

string, sewn into edges of backing to strengthen them

65

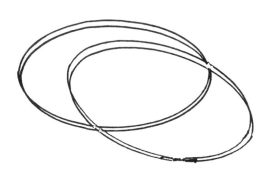

diagram 21a *Circular frame.*

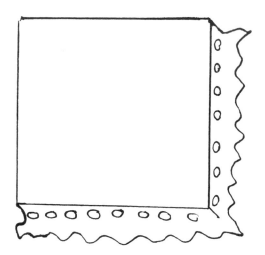

diagram 21b *A small square frame with the fabric attached by drawing pins.*

outwards. Always start from the centre and work outwards. When the material is flat and smooth, it is herringbone-stitched into position.

When working on a small square frame, the backing and the background fabric are tacked together and secured to the frame with drawing pins

(thumb tacks). One drawing pin is inserted in the centre of each side and then the embroiderer gradually works around the frame from these points, securing the fabric. The material is pulled taut as it is secured.

chapter six

Embroideries for the Ark

We have discussed the development of the synagogue as a meeting place for the faithful, where they gathered to hear the Reading of the Law. It has also been noted that the early synagogue did not contain a permanent Ark; the Ark was a portable chest which was carried in at the commencement of the service and out at the conclusion.

THE DEVELOPMENT OF THE ARK

The earliest Arks were wooden cupboards or chests, either cylindrical or rectangular, as can be seen on gilt glass cups from Roman times. They were, in fact, Roman bookcases in which the scrolls were lain horizontally upon shelves. The cylindrical form of Ark is shown in frescoes from the Dura Europos synagogue. A man can be seen reading from the scroll with a rounded box at his feet. The box is covered with a red cloth and its shape reminds one of the wooden tikkim used by contemporary Romaniote Jews as containers for the Torah. It is possible that the tikkim developed from this earliest form of Ark. Just as the ancient Ark of the Covenant was covered with a cloth when it was transported (Numbers 4:5, 6) these portable Arks were draped with a piece of fabric when they were carried in and out of the prayer hall.

There are two more features which can be noted from the Roman gilt-glass illustrations of the Holy Ark: sometimes traces of internal curtains are visible, and in other illustrations no curtain is visible at all. It can also be seen that the scrolls were usually unwrapped in early times, so it is possible that the curtain inside the Ark was used as a protection for the scrolls.

Fig. 46 *Roman gilt glass, third to fourth century. The open Ark is shown with the scrolls lying horizontally upon shelves. (Israel Museum, Jerusalem.)*

Fig. 47 *Mosaic floor from Beth Shean synagogue, sixth century. The Ark of the Covenant, with a parokhet before it and two menorot on either side are depicted. (Courtesy of the Israel Department of Antiquities and Museums.)*

THE TORAH-NICHE AND THE DEVELOPMENT OF THE PAROKHET

With the passage of time the custom of directing prayers out of the window towards Jerusalem changed, so that the Ark was placed against the wall nearest to Jerusalem and the congregation faced in this direction for prayer.

A special Torah-niche developed in which the Ark was placed. Remains of these can be seen in early synagogues. There are often holes in the wall above the Torah-niche which probably contained the fastenings for poles upon which the Ark curtain, the parokhet, hung. The mosaic floor of the Beth Shean Synagogue contains an illustration of what is probably an Ark with a parokhet hanging in front of it.

Different types of Ark curtain

The Ark curtain emphasizes the concept, which goes back to the Sanctuary in the desert, of separating areas of greater and lesser holiness. It also recalls the curtain that hung before the Holy of Holies in the Temple.

Some communities hang the parokhet behind the Ark doors and some congregations hang it in front. The position affects its visual impact upon the observer, and determines whether it dominates the Prayer Hall, or is simply part of the furnishings of the Ark. When the Ark curtain is hung inside the Ark, and is therefore only seen with the doors open, it is not a dominant feature of the Prayer Hall.

When hung outside the Ark, the curtain becomes the focal point. The Ark is always the central feature of the synagogue, and the embroidered curtain both draws attention to and conceals it.

The parokhet in Sephardi and Ashkenazi communities

The Sephardim hang the Ark curtain inside the Ark. It is said that this custom dates from the time when the 'New Christians', the Marranos, held clandestine synagogue services in Spain. They would have wished to conceal the presence of the Ark, so would not have hung a parokhet on the outside. However, it is possible that the custom harks back to more ancient times, as illustrated upon the Roman gilt-glass cups.

The Ashkenazi communities almost always have an external parokhet. Medieval prayer books show illustrations of the Ark in Ashkenazi synagogues with the parokhet attached to the Ark itself. It is possible that this was developed in order to enable swift removal during times of persecution. For whatever reason, the custom has persisted to the present day, and this is the form we recognize in an Ark and parochot belonging to an Ashkenazi community.

The Ark and parokhet in the Middle Ages

As we have seen, in ancient times the Torah scrolls were laid horizontally upon shelves in the Ark. At some point in antiquity this custom changed and the Ark became shallower and taller to accommodate the now vertically stored scrolls. This is how they are depicted in medieval manuscripts and prayer books. The Sarajevo Haggadah from fourteenth-century Spain has an illustration which shows an Ark with three scrolls placed upright within it, dressed in Torah mantles and decorated with Torah ornaments.

It is probable that the medieval parokhet carried no more elaborate decoration than an inscription.

The rabbinic injunction to write a beautiful scroll for Jewish ritual makes no mention of a beautiful parokhet. This omission is significant and leads one to believe that the parokhet was relatively plain and simple in the medieval period.

The collection of the Jewish Museum at Prague

Our greatest knowledge about antique parochot and Torah mantles comes from the collection of the Jewish Museum at Prague. Hana Volakova has analysed the collection in her highly informative book *Synagogue Treasures in Bohemia and Moravia*. It seems that contemporary fashions, both in ecclesiastical and secular circles, can be followed in the design of parochot and Torah mantles. Thus the Renaissance motif of a picture framed by architectural elements was adapted for use in the parokhet. The central picture area, known as the mirror, became either a beautiful piece of fabric, sometimes rare or antique, or a richly embroidered area. It was framed by heavily embroidered twisted pillars. The twisted-pillar motif was used when it reflected contemporary fashion and taste and not at other times.

Fabrics used for parochot

The range of fabrics employed in the past was very great. Gold and silver brocades, Spanish and Italian brocades, fine French and Italian silks were all used. A curtain in the Prague Museum collection dated 1842 was made of shot taffeta, with a design of Rococo garlands upon it. The use of red velvet with gold embroidery was favoured in the Baroque period. (It seems to have had a permanent effect upon synagogue embroideries.)

THE KAPPORET

The valance above the parokhet is called the *kapporet* after the gold mercy seat which rested upon the altar in the desert Sanctuary, and in the Temple. The valance probably developed for the sole purpose of covering the means of hanging the parokhet. It is not used with an internal Ark curtain and is not shown above the parokhet on the mosaic

Fig. 48 *Kapporet, Bohemia, Prague, 1867. White silk with woven checks of red, blue, green and brown. Hebrew inscription in gold thread: 'Holy unto the Lord'. (State Jewish Museum of Prague; photo: Whitworth Art Gallery.)*

from Beth Shean. The kapporet is not an item which the embroiderer should feel obliged to include, as it has little symbolic meaning and a relatively short Jewish history. In the past the kapporet was sometimes given by a different donor from the one who donated the Ark curtain. Its design did not necessarily reflect the design of the parokhet. It often contained five scallops which were decorated with the Temple implements. Dedicatory inscriptions were usually included.

EMBROIDERY FOR THE ARK IN DIFFERENT JEWISH COMMUNITIES

Italian Jewish ceremonial embroideries are very distinctive and can be easily identified. According to Cecil Roth, the Great Synagogue in Rome possessed an exceptionally lovely textile collection which was saved from the Nazis by a non-Jew who told the Nazi patrol that the door to the strong room was an emergency exit.

Bokharan synagogues contain two or three parochot for one Ark. As well as the curtain which hangs outside the Ark, one is hung inside and another behind the scrolls. These parochot are made from a variety of fabrics and do not contain embroidered details except for dedications.

All Arks are usually lined with fabric. The Thekkumbhagon Synagogue in Cochin, India, seems to have had an embroidered lining with dedicatory inscriptions, but this is unusual. Some modern synagogues in the United States have commissioned co-ordinating embroideries for the exterior and interior of the Ark and for the embroideries for the scrolls of the Law.

ARK CURTAINS FOR DIFFERENT OCCASIONS

Synagogues in the past often possessed different curtains for each day of the week – for Shabbat, the New Moon, Feast days and Fast days. There are still one or two synagogues which maintain a remnant of this custom and have parochot for various occasions. There is a synagogue which uses one curtain for Shabbat, one for weekdays, one for the festivals, another curtain for the New Year and the following Days of Penitence, and one special curtain for the Day of Atonement. The New West End

Fig. 49 *Interior of the Ark of the Thekkumbhagom Synagogue, Ernakulam Cochin, India. (Illustration from the 400th Anniversary Souvenir of the Cochin Synagogue, 18 December, 1968.)*

Fig. 50 *Interior of the Ark, Temple Beth Ami, Rockville MD. Joan Koslan Schwarz. Quilting and goldwork.*

Synagogue London uses one curtain for the High Holy Days and Shavuot, and the curtain in figure 9 for the period between the High Holy Days and Passover. A red curtain is used for the rest of the year.

The Brighton and Hove Hebrew Congregation use blue vestments for the pilgrim festivals of Succot, Shavuot and Pesach, red vestments for the rest of the year and white for the High Holy Days.

DESIGN CONSIDERATIONS FOR A PAROKHET

The embroiderer needs to consider whether the parokhet should drape like a curtain, or form a screen in front of the Ark. This will determine its design. A heavily embroidered curtain cannot hang

Fig. 51 *Silk parokhet with two columns and appliquéd lions on either side of an appliquéd crown. The valance is made of matching silk. (Hebrew Union College Skirball Museum, Los Angeles.)*

Fig. 52 *Parokhet; canvas embroidered with coloured silks and gold thread. Italian, 1703. (Victoria & Albert Museum, London)*

in graceful folds. The parochot from the past had very little extra fullness in them.

Designing a parokhet which hangs in folds

It is possible to design an embroidered and draped curtain in one of two ways:

1 A design of cords can be applied loosely to the folds of the curtain to form a pattern as in diagram 22.

2 The actual parokhet can be left clear of embroidery and the kapporet emphasized as in figure 53. In this case the kapporet, the pulls for the parokhet and the front of the desk cover for the bimah have all been designed as one unit.

Designing a parokhet as flat sliding screens

The parokhet can be treated as screens which will slide back away from the Ark instead of being pulled back in the conventional manner of drawing back a curtain. Figure 56 shows how a heavily embroidered

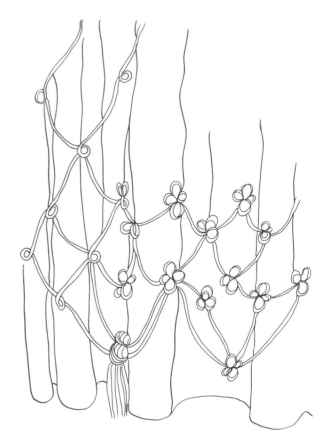

Fig. 53 *Padded appliqué kapporet by Ina Golub for Temple Beth El, Providence, Rhode Island. Indian silk on printed velvet, approximately 300 × 555 cm (10 × 18 ft). The pulls for the parokhet and the desk cover are made to form one design with the kapporet.*

diagram 22 *Cords loosely attached to the folds of the parokhet at the New West End Synagogue in such a way as to form a pattern.*

Fig. 54 *Parokhet by Pauline Brown; silk appliqué with embroidery in cotton perle, metal and rayon thread. 275 cm × 245 cm (9 × 8 ft). (New North London Synagogue.)*

Fig. 55 *Ark doors designed by Davie Hyman and worked by the sisterhood of the Temple Beth El, Ohio, in canvas work. The theme is the Creation.*

curtain can be made in this way (it is actually two curtains which part in the middle). The kapporet has been used to lift the eye above the curtains. The design reads from the bottom of the curtain and up through the kapporet into the space above the Ark.

EMBROIDERY APPLIED TO THE ARK DOORS

The curtain does not have to hang freely in front of the Ark, and embroiderers in the United States have applied the fabric to the Ark doors themselves (see figs 28, 55). In the case of the latter canvas work has been applied to the Ark doors. The kapporet has been used to enlarge the design and lift the eye above the Ark doors. This was part of a group project, designed by a professional and worked by members of the congregation.

JOINING FABRIC WIDTHS

It will usually be necessary to use more than one width of material when making a parokhet. Careful consideration has to be given to joining the fabric widths in order to achieve the best aesthetic results. Different solutions can be seen in various illustrations.

Traditionally, the parokhet was embroidered in sections and then assembled. In the traditional-style parokhet by Raphael Rothschild (fig. 56), appliqué strips of the Twelve Tribes have been used to cover the seams.

Fig. 56 *Parokhet for Shabbat by Raphael Rothschild with panels illustrating the Twelve Tribes. On the right side of the photograph another curtain can be seen, drawn to one side. This parokhet is used for weekdays and drawn aside for Shabbat.*

The parokhet for the New West End Synagogue has two equal widths of fabric with a seam running down the centre. The embroidered areas have been worked separately and then appliquéd to the curtain (see *fig. 9*).

WORKING ON AN ITEM AS LARGE AS A PAROKHET

It is not possible to apply the whole of the parokhet to an embroidery frame, as even if one had a room large enough, one would be unable to reach the middle of the embroidery. The curtain has to be worked in sections, each section being framed up in turn on calico. (The calico is cut away close to the embroidery afterwards.) The fabric which is not being worked is carefully rolled in tissue paper and tacked to the frame.

THE SIZE OF THE ARK

An Ark can be almost any size, from miniature to monumental. The Ark for the prayer hall of a synagogue will be large, but the synagogue may possess a small Ark for children's services and an even smaller travelling Ark for a house of mourning. Some individuals, both in the past and today,

Fig. 57 *An Ark from a farm in Russia; nineteenth century, approximately 60 cm (2 ft) high. (Private collection.)*

possess small personal Arks for private services in the home. Figure *57* shows an Ark which was made in Russia during the last century. It was used on a farm for the religious services of the farmer, his family and workers. Measuring approximately 60 cm (2 ft) high, it is fashioned in a style typical of Russian folk art of that period.

DESIGNING A PAROKHET FOR CHILDREN'S SERVICES

The embroiderer can experiment with a more modern and lively design for a parokhet for the children's services. As this curtain is not a permanent feature of the main synagogue prayer hall, a more unconventional style can be adopted. This may be a means of educating the public to be more adventurous in their attitude to embroidery.

MAKING UP A PAROKHET

Brief instructions on the making up of a parokhet are given below. The embroiderer is advised to study a specialist book on soft furnishings, such as *The Batsford Book of Soft Furnishings* by Angela Fishburn, to obtain all possible information which can be adapted to the making of synagogue vestments such as the parokhet, the desk covers or a chuppah.

The parokhet will need to be interlined to give the embroidery body, so it should be treated as an interlined curtain. Great care needs to be taken, when both pressing seams and 'locking' the interlining to the curtain, not to damage the embroidery.

1 The parokhet is cut out. Widths and half widths are joined with a flat seam and the seams pressed open. The widths and half widths are usually joined at the outside edge of the curtain.

2 The centre of the curtain is marked with a line of tacking. This facilitates the correct placement of details which have been embroidered separately and are to be appliquéd to the curtain.

3 Any areas which have been embroidered separately are appliquéd to the curtain at this point.

4 The interlining is made of domet or bump cloth. If the interlining has to be joined it will be necessary to make a lapped seam with a zigzag machine stitch, as the fabric tends to stretch.

5 The curtain is placed on a large, flat surface, with the wrong side upwards. The interlining is placed on top of the curtain and the sides and lower edges matched. The interlining is then folded back at the centre and 'locked' into position. Three rows of lockstitch are used every 120 cm (48 in.).

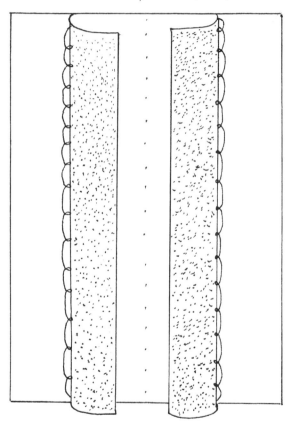

diagram 23 *'Locking' the lining to the top fabric.*

6 The curtain and interlining are turned in at the sides and bottom to form a hem of at least 5 cm (2 in.). Both fabrics are folded together, and tacked and herringbone-stitched into place. The corners will need to be mitred.

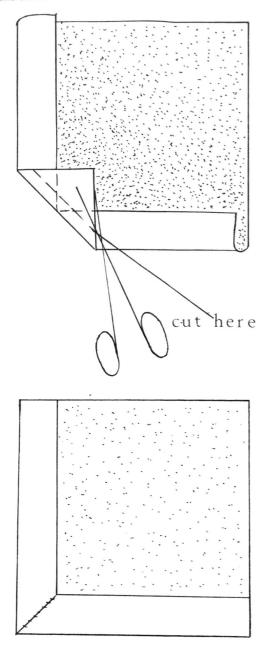

cut here

7 The lining is cut out to the same size as the curtain and widths and half widths joined in the same place as on the main curtain.

8 The lining is placed on top of the interlining, right side upwards, and 'locked' into position.

9 The side and bottom of the lining are turned and tacked and slipstitched to the curtain. The corners will need to be mitred.

10 The top of the curtain, interlining and lining fabrics are tacked together. The top is turned in and the heading is sewn on. The type of heading will differ according to the method of hanging the curtain.

diagrams 24, 25 *The mitred corner, two stages.*

chapter seven

Desk covers and pulpit falls

DESIGN CONSIDERATIONS

The reader conducts the service and reads the Torah from a desk on a raised area which is known as the *bimah*. The bimah is situated in a different part of the synagogue in an Orthodox synagogue as opposed to a Progressive synagogue. This can affect design considerations for the embroideries.

In the Orthodox synagogue, the bimah is situated in the centre of the building on the central axis in front of the Ark. The reader faces the Ark as he conducts the service. This is the position of the bimah as seen in illustrations from old prayer books and illuminated manuscripts over the ages. Often the pulpit will be situated in front of the Ark and opposite the bimah. The Ark itself is usually, but not

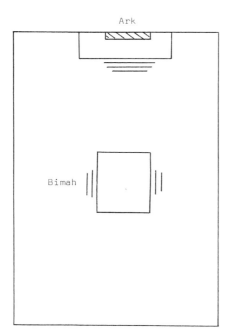

diagram 26 *Layout of the traditional orthodox synagogue.*

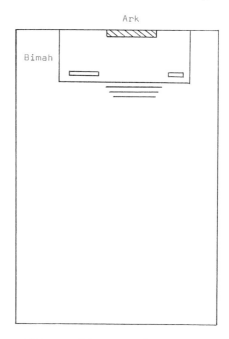

diagram 27 *Layout of the progressive synagogue.*

always, placed on a raised area in both Orthodox and Progressive synagogues.

In the Progressive synagogue the bimah is usually at the front of the prayer hall, next to the Ark. The raised area around the Ark becomes, in effect, a stage, with the reader conducting the service facing the congregation. In some synagogues another desk is placed parallel to the reader's desk on the other side of the Ark. The arrangement of the bimah and the area surrounding the Ark as one unit facing the congregation produces a more formal and dramatic format, with an unimpeded view of the Ark. (There may be Progressive synagogues with a centrally placed bimah facing the Ark, but I do not know of any.)

A COVER FOR THE READER'S DESK

As the Torah scrolls are very holy, it is forbidden to place them directly upon the desk top; a desk cover is always used (with the exception of the 9 Av). In ancient times, when the Ark was a portable chest, it was carried into the prayer hall draped with a cloth. It appears that when the scroll was read, the cloth was draped over the desk. In time a more formal desk cover was developed.

Matching parochot and desk covers

Because some synagogues had different parochot for all the festivals – for each day of the week, the Sabbath, fast days and the new moon – it seems probable that whilst a number may have had matching desk covers, this would not necessarily have been the case. The sources which refer to parochot for different occasions do not mention matching desk covers. The conventional synagogue today usually has desk covers to match the parochot: one set for the majority of the year, and one set for the High Holy Days. Of the synagogues I know which keep up the custom of different parochot for different occasions, some have matching desk covers and others do not. I think that one can therefore draw the conclusion that the designer and community should choose whichever system suits them best; there is no hard and fast rule.

When I designed the desk covers in colour plate 4 I wanted the fabric to harmonize with the gold colour of the wood of the bimah area rather than with the dark green of the Ark curtains. Appliquéd details pick up the colours of the curtains, the stained-glass windows and the hangings, thus creating a unified design within the context of the whole prayer hall.

Embroidering different areas of the desk cover

A desk cover can be embroidered on the front, or on three or four sides, and perhaps on the top too. If the craftsperson wishes to embroider the top, practicality must be considered. This is the working area; it is used for rolling and unrolling the scrolls, both during the services and when the scrolls are prepared in advance. It can also be the desk where the bride and groom sign the wedding register. Care must be taken not to use embroidery techniques which could damage the parchment of the scrolls. Some metal threads would be best avoided (although metal-thread embroidery has been used in the past). One must also bear in mind the considerable wear the embroidery will receive. Long, loose threads, purls, beads and sequins are probably impractical.

A greater variety of techniques, which can include more delicate fabrics and a wider range of stitchery, can be considered for the sides of the desk cover.

Different shapes of desk covers

The desk cover can be a throw, or a fitted cover with shaped corners. The style will depend upon the congregation for whom it is made, and upon the designer.

Desk covers have varied in the past from synagogue to synagogue depending upon the wealth, sophistication and taste of the community. Figure *58* shows a cover which is shaped, but not fitted. The sides hang loosely over the sides of the desk, and are not secured.

Fig. 58 *Desk cover for the Hambro Synagogue, London, 1830–40. White ribbon silk embroidered with silk chenille and gold and silver threads. The embroidery may have come from Austria. (Jewish Museum, London.)*

Fig. 59 *Hanging for the reader's desk. Canvas embroidered with coloured silks and gold thread with floral inscriptions and emblems; Italy, 1703. (Victoria & Albert Museum, London.)*

Desk covers and pulpit falls

Working the embroidery upon a separate, removable piece of fabric

As the desk cover receives regular wear, it is worth considering working the embroidery upon a separate piece of fabric which can be placed over the desk cover. This is only practical if the embroidered area is confined to the front, but it does have advantages; it means that the fabric which is embroidered need not be the same as the material for the desk cover. Plate 4 and the front cover illustration show desk covers for the North Western Reform Synagogue, London, which were designed in this way. The embroidery is worked upon silk which would not be suitable for the desk top as it would crease easily. The desk covers were made of velvet, in a colour to match the silk. The embroideries were attached to a separate piece of velvet which was draped over the desk. An iron bar

at the back acts as a counterbalance for the weighty metal thread embroidery. (It is sewn into a piece of calico, which forms an extra interlining throughout the whole embroidery, to take the strain of the embroidery and the iron bar.) The above method allows for the desk covers to be replaced as necessary, without the embroidery being lost.

Pat Russell has used a different solution for the High Holy Day desk covers for the Liberal Synagogue, St John's Wood, London. Here the actual tops of the desk covers are made separately, of a more durable material, and are attached to the embroidered 'skirts' when the covers are used.

Instructions for making a fitted desk cover

1 Measure desk.

2 Cut out and tack up the lining of the desk cover to make sure it fits. Cut out the front, the top and the back in one piece, and then cut out the two side panels, making sure that the grain runs in the same direction throughout, with the selvedge running the length of the material.

3 Pin, tack and machine the side pieces to the top. Press the seams open. Snip the seam allowance as shown in diagram *28* to facilitate making a sharp corner.

4 Cut out the fabric for the bimah cover and make up in the same way. Synagogue committees will often ask for velvet, but remember that this is a particularly hard fabric to machine and there will be seams where the two sections will have to be joined with the pile running in opposite directions. It will be necessary to put tissue, or even brown paper, between the layers of fabric to prevent them puckering.

5 Lay the lining against the desk cover, with the seams facing inward. Catch the lining and the desk cover together along all the seams.

6 Turn up the hem of the desk cover. Turn up the hem of the lining and catch to the cover.

If a lightweight fabric is used, interlining will be necessary.

Fig. 60 *Desk cover for the High Holy Days by Pat Russell for the Liberal Jewish Synagogue, London. The design is of the burning bush. It is one of a pair; the other cover depicts the menorah.*

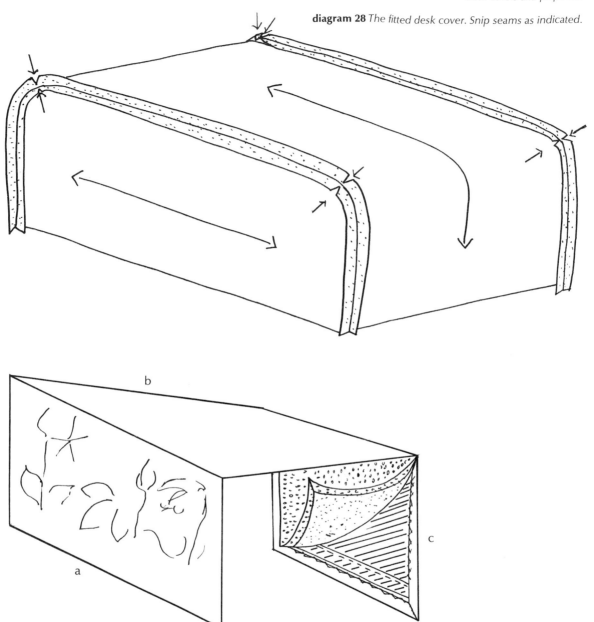

diagram 28 *The fitted desk cover. Snip seams as indicated.*

diagram 29 *The embroidery for the desk cover is attached to a separate piece of fabric which hangs over the desk cover. (a) Embroidered front of desk cover; (b) velvet hanging for top and back; (c) calico strip which runs the full length of the piece (with pocket for iron bar) and is slipped into the velvet at the sides but hangs free of the bottom hem.*

Instructions for making a separate piece attached to the embroidery, which is placed over the desk cover

1 Cut out a piece of calico the full width and length, from the bottom edge of the embroidery to the edge of the backdrop, plus an allowance for turnings and hems.

2 Cut out a piece of heavyweight, non-woven interlining (such as non-fusable *Vilene* [Pellon] or deckchair canvas), the exact size of the embroidery. Herringbone-stitch in place to the calico.

3 Turn in the sides and front edges of the calico, and herringbone-stitch to the interfacing. Turn in the side and front edges of the embroidery and herringbone stitch to the calico.

4 Cut out a piece of the fabric which has been used for the desk cover, with the grain running in the same direction as it does for the desk cover, and in the same direction as the embroidered fabric. Tack and machine to the top edge of the embroidered fabric.

5 Tack the calico almost the full length of the top fabric but leave enough material to make a deep hem which will form a pocket for the iron bar.

6 Turn in the sides of the top fabric and calico and herringbone-stitch into place, leaving a gap at the edge for the iron bar to lie comfortably within the side hems.

7 Cover an iron bar, which has been cut to size, with plastic film and tape to make sure it does not rust and mark the fabric; alternatively, paint the iron bar with rust-proofer and paint. Make a deep hem in the calico and slip the iron bar into it. Sew up the sides of the pocket.

8 Lay the calico and the iron bar inside the side hem of the top fabric. It should not reach as far as the hem, as this would disturb the lie of the material. Turn up the bottom and hem. It will be necessary to mitre the corners.

PULPIT FALLS

Orthodox synagogues have a separate pulpit, but in Progressive synagogues the rabbi usually preaches from the same desk which has been used to conduct the service and read the Law. The majority of pulpit falls in contemporary synagogues are very simple, often little more than a piece of fabric embroidered with a Star of David and draped over the pulpit. They are usually made of the same material as the desk cover and the parokhet. Some synagogues do not have pulpit falls at all. They are not usually considered to be as important a feature as the desk cover and the parokhet which are the main focal areas. Colour plate 5 shows a beautiful pulpit fall from the Spanish and Portuguese Jews Congregation in London. It depicts the Tree of Life, and is used for the High Holy Days. This synagogue possesses many magnificent sets of vestments, with matching parochot, desk covers and pulpit falls, and covers for the Torah scroll.

Fig. 61 *Pulpit fall depicting the Tree of Life by Estelle Levy for the Spanish and Portuguese Jews Congregation, London. Silk appliqué, jap gold and silk-embroidered lettering, some gold kid.*

Brief instructions for making a pulpit fall

Some of the pulpit falls in synagogues in Britain today drape over both the front and the back of the pulpit. The pulpit fall in colour plate 5 is secured by being partly draped over the rabbi's side of the pulpit and by having two ties with *Velcro* (touch-and-close fastener) which are caught underneath. There is no standard shape or design for a synagogue pulpit, so the embroiderer will need to examine the fall in current use and take the shape from that. It will need interlining such as *Vilene (Pellon)* if a firm shape is required, or perhaps with calico for a softer outline. The embroiderer should realize that the synagogue will be very conscious of avoiding any shape or design which could be interpreted as not Jewish.

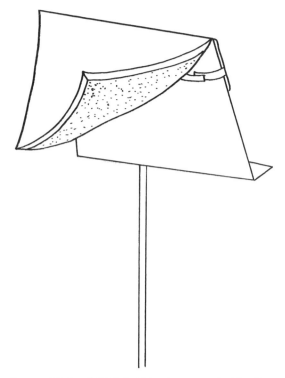

diagram 30 *A pulpit fall, held by ties secured with velcro.*

85

chapter eight

Embroideries for the Scrolls of the Law

Embroidered wrappings for the Torah scroll were used in antiquity. The public reading of the Torah dates from the time of the first synagogues. The Torah has always been handwritten upon parchment, but in the early days the Torah consisted of a number of different scrolls. They were stored, as all contemporary scrolls were, horizontally in a portable chest, which the Jews called the Ark.

In time, the scrolls were amalgamated to form one unit and this was the officially approved form by the fourth century CE. The use of damaged scrolls has always been forbidden and the amalgamated scrolls were bulkier, and needed greater care in handling. Their height was increased to accommodate the greater width, and wooden staves or pillars were sewn on to each end. (The custom of sewing in staves or pillars was in general use at this time, although there were differences in the customs for rolling the Torah.)

Each stave, or pillar, is known as an *Etz Hayim*, Tree of Life. The pillars were often carved and even today one can find scrolls with the Etzei Hayim decorated with inlaid mother of pearl or ivory, and beautifully carved. Occasionally the Etzei Hayim were made of silver. (See *fig. 3* which shows a small scroll with silver Etzei Hayim.)

The next stage in the development of the Torah scroll was for round flanges to be attached to each end of the rod to prevent the parchment slipping and to facilitate the rolling and unrolling of the scrolls. In the past, silver inscriptions were sometimes attached to the flange, giving the name of the donor and the date of the donation.

Gradually, silk wrappings were used to protect the scrolls, in the same way that contemporary heathen scrolls were wrapped. Both the Talmud and Josephus discuss the embroidered wrappings for the Torah (Sabbath 133b, Kelim 25:5). The schools of Hillel and Shammai (20–50 CE) discussed the suitability of various embroidered wrappings, giving rulings on which were to be considered clean and which unclean. It is possible that the embroidered wrappings go back even further, there are some fragments from the Dead Sea Scrolls which suggest the custom was already being followed at the time of the Hasmoneans (175–140 BCE). There are records of craftsmen working on wrappings for the Torah in the home of Judah ha-Nasi (200 CE), the editor of the *Mishna*.

It seems probable that the development of mantles must have come about when the scrolls were placed upright in the Ark, as wrappings would have slipped down. The use of flanges must also have had a bearing on the development of the mantle; they would have made it easier to hang a cover over the scroll without damaging the parchment. Thus the fabric coverings for the scroll came to be divided into two distinct items, the mantle, and the wrapper or binder which held the scroll firmly and securely beneath the mantle. By this time the scroll had become an imposing visual symbol which looked impressive when it was removed from the Ark and carried around the synagogue in ceremonial procession before and after the reading of the Law.

The word 'mantle' is believed by some people to refer to the outer garment worn by the High Priest in the Temple. However, the Romans called the covers for their scrolls by a similar name. The wrapper was referred to in antiquity as the *mappah* which is a word used in the Bible to describe a shawl-like garment (Isaiah 3:22, Ruth 3:15). In later times mapah was used to describe a wrapper of up to 20 cm (8 in.) wide and *mitpahat* was used if the wrapper covered the full width of the scroll.

DEVELOPMENTS IN THE WRAPPINGS FOR THE SCROLLS

In ancient times, bells were sewn on to the cloth which wrapped the Torah scroll. The Talmud discusses which bells were to be considered clean and which unclean (Sab. 58b). Modern Yemenite Jews have a custom which may come from this ancient practice. It is the custom for a kerchief, which often has hollow bell-shaped ornaments sewn on to the hem, to be tied to the wooden *tik*. (In connection with the fabric adornment of the tiks of Romaniote Jews, one should also mention that in Bokharan communities the women consider it a great honour to give to the synagogue brightly coloured scarves which are then tied to the tik.) The attachment of bells to the wrappings for the Torah is interesting. Exodus 28 describes bells being attached to the priestly robes; could the custom derive from this passage? Today bells are not attached to the Torah wrappings in European synagogues, but they do form part of the ornaments for the finials which decorate the Torah staves.

There are records from the twelfth century of women leaving Torah cloaks to the congregation. (The earliest *Memorbuch of Nuremberg*). In Italy, special blessings were formulated for the women who made the cloaks and wraps for the Torah scrolls.

Fig. 62 *Tik cover in canvas work by Sharon Norry for Congregation Beth El, Rochester, New York.*

Illuminated manuscripts from the Middle Ages show that the Torah mantles were very different from those to which we are accustomed today. In illustrations from the second half of the fifteenth century both Italian and German mantles are shown resting on the top of the Etzei Hayim. The Italian mantle is depicted as being completely open up the side and two tassels are stitched at the join of the back and front. The German mantles appear to be more like inverted narrow bags with a slit at the bottom to reveal a portion of the scroll beneath.

By the end of the Middle Ages brocaded fabrics were manufactured specifically for the Torah mantles and became an important part of ritual art. The general design of the mantles varied from country to country as it does to this day. Italian communities used a mantle which was narrow at the top and wider at the bottom. German communities tended to use a straighter design. Jews from Eastern Europe hung their mantles from narrow straps over the Torah scroll, like vests.

Sephardi communities used much fuller and looser mantles with one opening up the back, like a dress, and the Romaniote communities which used a tik, sometimes placed a mantle over the tik. The seventeenth and eighteenth centuries saw more elaborately embroidered mantles and particularly beautiful mantles were made for both the Ashkenazi and Sephardi communities in England. These mantles often employed rich stumpwork in their designs.

TORAH ORNAMENTS

Torah ornaments are worth discussing in greater detail as they affect the embroideries for the scrolls.

Two types of ornaments are used for the staves of the scrolls: *rimmonim*, which fit individually upon each stave, and a Torah crown, which fits over both staves. The other ornament is the *yad*, or pointer which hangs down from the Etzei Hayim. Records from the sixteenth century show that the yad was not used at that time. A cloth was placed upon the scroll and moved downwards when the reader chanted. This was to prevent the fingers of the reader touching the parchment of the scroll and

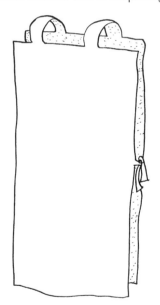

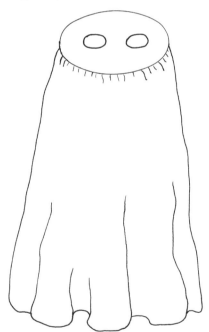

diagrams 31, 32, 33 *Three different shaped Torah mantles: 31 from Ashkenazi Eastern Europe; 32 from Ashkenazi Germany; 33 from Sephardi communities.*

possibly leaving grease-marks on it or damaging it. In the seventeenth and eighteenth centuries, pointers were developed for this purpose. There is no reason why the pointer has to hang in front of the mantle, but it is usual in many communities for it to do so. Some congregations, such as the Spanish and Portuguese Jews Congregation in London, tuck the yad into the binder under the mantle rather than hanging it from the Etzei Hayim.

There are occasions, such as festivals and the new moon, when two scrolls are removed from the Ark for the reading of the Law during the synagogue service. Occasionally three scrolls are used. The custom developed, during the sixteenth century, of hanging a small plaque from the Etzei Hayim, to

inform the reader which scroll had been prepared for which portion of the Law. During the seventeenth and eighteenth centuries, large ornamental plaques were developed, with removable pieces which could be changed to show which portion each scroll had been turned to. They came to be known as breastplates, after the breastplate worn by the High Priest in the Temple, but there is no religious reason for using them. They have never been used in Sephardi communities, which still retain the small plaque to differentiate the scrolls, and they are not used by Liberal Jewish communities.

This particular Torah ornament is of great interest to the embroiderer as it obscures so much of the embroidery upon the mantle. When designing a Torah mantle, it is necessary to ascertain whether a breastplate will be used. If a community insists upon its use, the embroiderer will have to bear this in mind when designing the mantle. Figure 63 shows mantles

Fig. 63 *Festive Torah mantles by Ina Golub; white raw silk appliquéd with iridescent and solid dupion silks and silk brocade. Hand-tied fringe, metallic braids, ribbons, cords, pearls and bells. (Temple B'nai Abraham, Livingston, New Jersey.)*

which have been designed to accommodate a breastplate.

In the past some impoverished communities which were unable to afford silver Torah ornaments made them of tin or wood or sometimes of brocade. Today, many communities are concerned about theft from the synagogue. Some synagogues in the United States have commissioned embroidered Torah headpieces instead of silver ones.

STYLISTIC DIFFERENCES BETWEEN ASHKENAZI AND SEPHARDI MANTLES TODAY

The Ashkenazi mantle consists of a tube, usually made of two pieces of material, a front and a back, attached to a hard top. There are usually vents left open at the base of each side seam to facilitate the dressing and undressing of the Torah scroll.

The Sephardi mantle is fuller and has a central opening up the back. It is softly gathered on to the hard top and is often made of silk. Pale blues, pinks and purples are all used for the mantles in sharp contrast to the red and blue velvets which dominate many contemporary Ashkenazi synagogues.

The backs of the Sephardi mantles are often richly embroidered, with the embroidery framing the central back opening. The scrolls are usually placed in the Ark with the back showing so that they can be taken out of the Ark and handed to the person who is to carry them without having to be turned round. This has led to confusion about the design of the mantles, with people thinking that the central opening is up the front.

Today, as in the past, in Sephardi communities a piece of coloured silk is wrapped around the back of the scroll, so that when the scroll is raised during the service, the parchment at the back is concealed by the backing. The backing is usually chosen in a colour which tones with the binder and the Torah mantle. (Sometimes in the past a special piece of embroidery was made to hook on to the back of the open scroll when it was raised and displayed to the congregation.)

Even when I am making an Ashkenazi-style mantle, I prefer to use the central back opening as

Fig. 64 *Torah mantle on the theme of 'Earth' by Linda Price. Cornelli machine embroidery on to a honey-coloured velvet ground. Patched and pieced leather, silk and velvet, trapunto quilting, machine and hand embroidery, hand beading.*

Fig. 65 *Torah mantle, early eighteenth century, brocade in gold and silver thread and coloured silks. Metal thread embroidery. (Spanish and Portuguese Jews Congregation, London.)*

Fig. 66 *Torah mantle by Constance Howard MBE. Wool and synthetic fibres, hand appliqué with machine-couched gold and black chenille thread. (Property of the Embroiderers' Guild.)*

this allows the skirt of the mantle to be made in one piece.

To my knowledge, the Eastern European style mantle with straps is no longer used today.

THE SIZE OF THE SCROLL

Scrolls vary greatly in size. They can be very small, for domestic use, or very large indeed. In theory each scroll should be measured when a mantle is commissioned and the mantle made for that particular scroll. The reality is that synagogue officials swap around the mantles. Although the mantle will never fit scrolls which vary greatly in size, one has to accept that one can make a mantle to fit a specific scroll perfectly and find it used upon a different scroll for which it is either too big or too small.

Fig. 67 *Miniature Torah mantle for a sixteenth-century Venetian Torah. Silk brocade, metallic braid, rayon rattail, bells and beads, 32 cm (12½ in.) high. (Ina Golub for Temple B'nai Abraham, Livingston, New Jersey.)*

FABRIC FOR TORAH MANTLES

As has already been discussed, Torah mantles receive very hard wear because of the regular dressing and undressing of the Torah scroll during the synagogue service. Materials for Torah mantles should be able to stand up to robust treatment and should not crease easily. When the scroll is carried around the synagogue in procession, the person carrying it may be nervous and tense (he is always an ordinary member of the congregation, not an official); he may well clutch the cover with hot, sticky hands, and it is no use using a fabric which cannot stand up to this treatment. The metal Torah ornaments too (the breastplate and yad) may have edges which could pull and snag delicate materials.

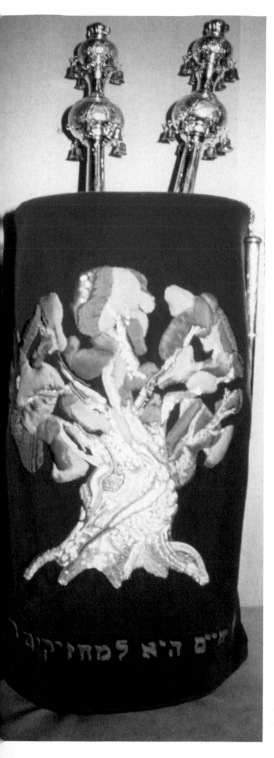

Torah mantle by Kathryn Salomon on the theme *of the Tree of Life. Velvet with silk appliqué and metal thread embroidery. (The North Western Reform Synagogue, London)*

2 *Torah mantle by Kathryn Salomon on the theme of 'Living Water'; velvet with silk appliqué and metal thread embroidery. (The North Western Reform Synagogue, London)*

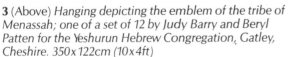

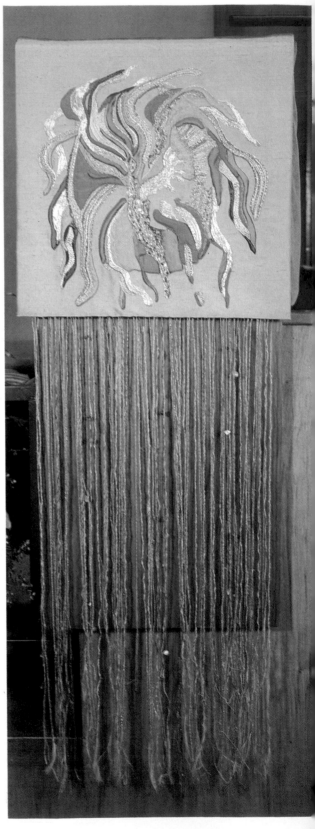

3 (Above) *Hanging depicting the emblem of the tribe of Menassah; one of a set of 12 by Judy Barry and Beryl Patten for the Yeshurun Hebrew Congregation, Gatley, Cheshire. 350 x 122cm (10 x 4ft)*

4 *Small desk cover by Kathryn Salomon on the theme of 'Choose Life' from Deuteronomy. Silk appliqué, silk and metal thread embroidery, beads and spangles on a silk ground. One of a pair for the North Western Reform Synagogue, London. 41 x 41cm (16 x 16in.). Because the desks were so different in size the design was balanced by means of the fringes. The large cover has a small fringe and the small cover has a very long fringe enriched with beads.*

5 (Above) *Pulpit fall by Estelle Levy
on the theme of the Tree of Life. Silk
appliqué, jap gold, and silk
embroidered lettering, some gold kid.*
(Spanish and Portuguese Jews
Congregation, London)

6 (Above) *Chuppah by Temma Gentles; polyester, silk,
cotton cord. Each side of the triangles measures 550cm (6ft).*
(Temple Emanu-El, Toronto)

7 (Above) *Kippah for Passover; grey wool with gold thread and leather, by Estelle Levy, London. The four cups of wine which are drunk symbolically during the Seder Service are depicted upon the kippah.*
(Property of Rabbi Levy)

8 (Left) *Kippah by Esther Carvalho, London; silk and metal thread embroidery and sequins upon reversed satin.* (Property of Mr R. N. Carvalho)

9 (Opposite) *The open Ark at the North Western Reform Synagogue, London. In the front row are Torah mantles by Kathryn Salomon on the themes of the Tree of Life and 'Living Water'. They are made of velvet with silk appliqué and silk and metal thread embroidery. The flame the Tree of Life and water, the symbols used in the front row of Torah scrolls, are universal and speak to all people. Note the Torah ornaments, the rimonim, the Torah crown, the pointers and the breastplates (these can be seen in the back row).*

10 (Opposite) *Ark doors designed by Davie Hyman and worked by the sisterhood of the Temple Beth El, Ohio. Canvas work embroidery. The theme is the Creation.*

11 *Ark curtain depicting the Temple and the menorah. New West End Synagogue, London, designed by Alfred Cohen and embroidered by the Royal School of Needlework.*

12 *Tallit by Ina Golub. Wool with organza appliqué.*

13 *Tik cover in canvas work by Sharon Norry for Congregation Beth El, Rochester, New York.*

STANDS FOR TORAH MANTLES DURING THE SYNAGOGUE SERVICE

As the mantle is removed from the scroll during the service, it is worth investigating the way in which the mantle will be hung when it is taken off the scroll. Some communities who do not consider the care of their mantles in any depth may have inadequate methods of keeping the mantles during this period. They may be folded up and left on a seat, and so could be pushed around or crushed during the reading of the Law. Diagrams 34, 35 and 36 show stands employed at a number of synagogues. If the system at a particular synagogue is inadequate and will lead to the misuse of the mantles, perhaps the embroiderer may be able to suggest a suitable method.

MAKING A TORAH MANTLE

Modern Torah mantles are made with a hard top. The two flanges at the top of the scroll must be measured to ascertain the size. A pattern is cut in cardboard and placed over the scroll to make sure it fits before the final board is cut out. The Torah scroll is read from one end and through the year gradually rolled towards the other end. The two rollers are rolled towards the middle. This means that the size of each side of the scroll gradually changes during the year. At the beginning the majority of the parchment is on one roller, and by the end of the year the majority of the parchment is on the other roller. Only in the middle of the year will there be an equal amount of parchment on each roller. The holes must be large enough to allow for the changing size of each side of the scroll, but not so large that the mantle flops about when the scroll is in use. In fact this is not as difficult a problem as it sounds, but the changing shape must be borne in mind.

It is surprising how different the tops of the Etzei Hayim can be. The handles of the rollers can be carved; some have bulbous shapes which can prevent the mantle from lying correctly upon the flanges, and so make the mantle appear shorter

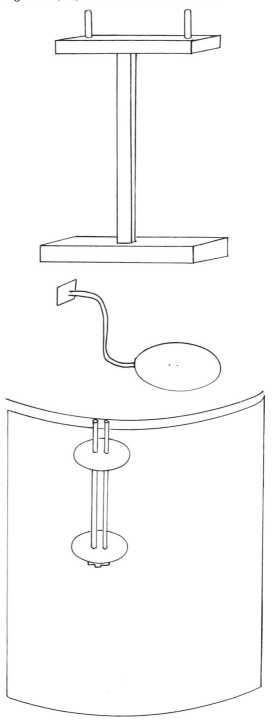

diagrams 34, 35, 36 *Stands for Torah mantles.*

when it is placed upon the scroll. It is therefore necessary to remove the mantle which is already clothing the scroll when fitting the hard top; it is no use fitting it over the mantle as this may prove deceptive (see *fig. 70*).

The hard top should be made of hardboard or plywood. If plywood is used, the edges will need to be sanded down to make them smooth.

There are a number of methods of assembling the components of a Torah mantle and two are given below.

Method 1

1 The hard top is covered with a soft material such as domett. The holes are cut-out and stitched. Place the lining above and below the board and stitch around it. Cut the surplus fabric away from the inside of the holes, leaving 1.5 cm ($\frac{3}{4}$ in.) seam allowance. Nick the seam allowance, so that it can be turned inwards. Trim excess if necessary and stitch.

2 Mark the centre front, centre back and side points of the hard top.

3 Cut out a piece of the mantle fabric, large enough to cover the top, allowing 2 cm (1 in.) seam allowance. Make sure that the grain of the fabric runs in the same direction as that on the 'skirt'. Mark the centre front, the centre back and the side points. A light interfacing will be necessary if a lightweight fabric is used.

4 Lay the fabric over the hard top and mark the shape and position of the holes.

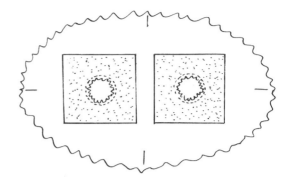

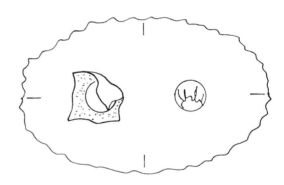

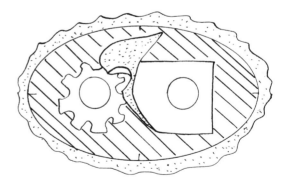

diagrams 37, 38, 39, 40 *Making facings for the holes in the hard top of a Torah mantle.*

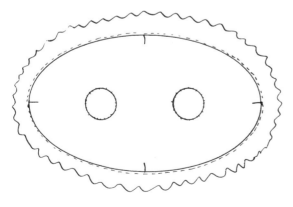

5 Cut two squares of the mantle fabric, on the cross, to make facings for the holes. They will probably need to be approximately 13 cm (5 in.) square, although they may well need to be trimmed down later.

6 Place the right side of the square to the right side of the top fabric, tack and machine twice. Cut away the material from the centre of the hole, leaving a seam allowance of approximately 1.5 cm ($\frac{3}{4}$ in.). Snip seam allowance carefully. Repeat with the other hole.

7 Place the top fabric of the mantle over the hard top, matching the centre front, back and side points. Turn the hole facings through the holes and pull through to the underside of the hard top. The fabric will need to be cut to allow the facing to lie flat and must be sewn to the lining material on the underneath of the hard top. Repeat with the other hole. If desired, a rectangular piece of fabric can be sewn over the raw edges on the underneath of the hard top to give a smooth finish.

8 Cut out the lining for the 'skirt'.

9 Matching the centre front, the side points and the centre back, tack the lining and then machine to the seam allowance of the hard top, as close to the hard area as possible. The seam down the centre back will need to be caught by hand for approximately 14–15 cm (6 in.).

10 Take the top fabric for the mantle 'skirt' and match the centre front, the side points and the centre back to the equivalent points on the top piece. Tack and stitch. Care is needed when turning the mantle to the right side before catching the seam at the back. Metal thread embroidery will crack if it is bent, so the hard top will need to be manoeuvred adroitly. (This sounds harder than it is – just be careful to bend the embroidery as little as possible.) Once again the centre back seam will need to be caught for about 14–15 cm (6 in.).

11 Attach the lining to the top fabric down the long open vent at the back of the mantle.

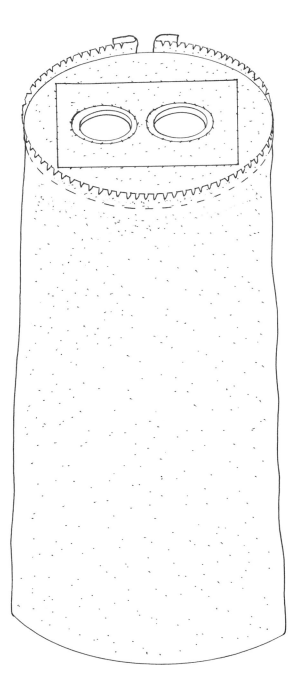

diagram 41 *Applying the 'skirt' to the hard top.*

12 Whenever possible, the mantle should be placed upon the designated scroll, preferably *in* the Ark, to ensure that the hem is made the correct length before any final stitching is undertaken. The mantle is best looked at in the Ark, if possible, because the length needs to be right for the scroll, and the height from the floor of the Ark should be similar to that of the other scrolls. The amount of the Etzei Hayim which is allowed to show below the mantle is a purely aesthetic consideration, but when a number of scrolls are seen inside the Ark, the lengths of the mantles in relation to the rollers should be similar.

13 Hem the mantle; the corners will need to be mitred. Turn up the lining and attach to the inside of the hem.

The above method is undoubtedly far more time-consuming and fiddly than the one which follows. However, it does ensure that the mantle has a smooth, neat top seam where the 'skirt' joins the hard top. A seam which will not need to be concealed in any way.

Method 2
The method used by commercial firms is much simpler and quicker. The disadvantage is that the seam at the top of the mantle, where the 'skirt' joins the hard top, is ugly and needs to be concealed. Many people cover the seam with upholstery braids or fringes, but this usually looks crude and ugly as so many braids and fringes are far too heavy. They can spoil an otherwise lovely piece of work. Great care and ingenuity needs to be taken in finding a suitable method of concealing this seam. A braid or fringe could be made of the embroidery materials used in the mantle, or a rouleau could be made of the same fabric as the mantle and sewn over the seam. This will need to be considered when the fabric for the mantle is bought and sufficient material purchased.

Covering the hard top
1 The hard top is covered with a soft material such as domett. The holes are cut out of the domett and the edges finished.

diagram 42 *The completed Torah mantle with the opening up the back. (The seam is caught for a few inches at the top from the right side.)*

2 A piece of lining material is placed underneath the hard top, a piece of the top fabric over it, right side upwards, and the two are stitched together.

3 The holes are cut leaving 1.5 cm ($\frac{3}{4}$ in.) seam allowance, turned and finished. (Braid can be used to cover these seams around the inside of the holes.)

4 The centre front, centre back and side points are marked.

96

Making the skirt

It is best to make the whole skirt in one piece with a central back opening, as this allows the mantle to be made up without turning the embroidery inside out.

1 Cut out a piece of the lining material the same size as the top fabric. Tack the two materials together on three sides, (the hem is made later). The centre front, centre back and side points of the 'skirt' are matched up with those points on the hard top and then they are slipstitched together by hand.

2 The lining is attached to the top fabric down the long open vent at the back of the mantle.

3 The seam at the centre back is caught by hand and the hem turned up.

An Ashkenazi-style mantle is usually made with front and back of the 'skirt' made of separate pieces, and a seam down each side. There are vents at the bottom of each side seam to facilitate the dressing and undressing of the scroll. This method can only be used with any embroidery which will not be damaged by turning the whole skirt area inside out.

TORAH BINDERS

Joseph Gutman has written a detailed account of this tradition. The Torah binder, *mappah* or *wimpel* (different names are used in different parts of the world) is an interesting item. Throughout its history it has been associated with the personal dedications of the ordinary members of the community, not just the rich and influential. The custom has varied from country to country.

The origin of the wrapper has already been described in connection with the development of the Torah mantle; it is probably the most ancient form of decoration for the Torah scroll.

The wimpel from Germany

The custom of dedicating a wimpel on the first occasion a boy was taken to the synagogue seems to have originated in Southern Germany, in Bavaria, around 1500. It is mentioned by Antonius Margaritia in his book about Judaism, *The Entire Jewish Faith*, published in 1530. Apparently the binder was often made from the swaddling clothes of a baby boy. It was embroidered by the mother or another close female relative such as the grandmother, an unmarried girl or a bride, but it could also have been made professionally.

The inscription followed a prescribed formula:

. . . . [Hebrew name of the child], son of . . . . [Hebrew name of the father], may he live long and happily [or, may his Rock [God] guard him and keep him in life], born under a good constellation [the constellation corresponding to the month the child was born] on [the day of the week, Hebrew date, month and year], may he grow [or, may the Lord cause him to grow, or may the Lord make him worthy to grow] to [study of] Torah, to get married [chuppah] and to [perform] good deeds. Amen, Selah.

The lettering was often drawn by a professional Torah scribe, or a cantor who also worked as a scribe, and then embroidered by someone else. In later times wimpels were frequently painted and not embroidered.

The German wimpel was usually linen, even if it was not made from the swaddling clothes. It was made of a square piece of material cut into four separate pieces which were later sewn together to form a long strip measuring 2–4 metres (approximately 2–4 yards). Sometimes the edge of the linen was bound with silk, and occasionally in rich families the complete wimpel was made of silk. This gave rise to a popular saying: 'on the birth of . . . .'s child you could hear the silk rustle'.

The lettering reflected contemporary Hebrew illuminated manuscripts and was decorated with floral, animal and bird motifs. People were represented holding the Torah or beneath the chuppah wearing contemporary clothes.

The binder was presented to the synagogue on the first visit of the child to the synagogue somewhere between one month and three years. If he was older, he would help his father bind the Torah scroll after the reading of the Law. The wimpel was used again for his barmitzvah.

Fig. 68 *Torah binder. Silk embroidery on linen Alsace, dated 1719–20. (Victoria & Albert Museum, London.)*

Fig. 69 *Torah binder from Trinidad, Colorado, 1889. Undyed linen, polychrome pigments and silk threads. (Hebrew Union College Skirball Museum, Los Angeles.)*

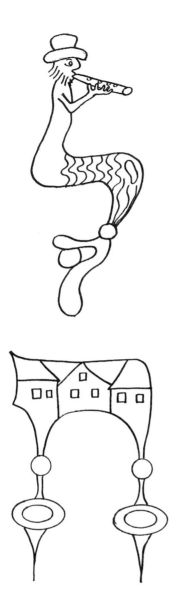

diagrams 43, 44 *Painted lettering from a nineteenth century wimpel in the Israel Museum.*

This charming custom resulted in a birth registry for all the male children of a given community. Before its destruction by the Nazis, Worms Synagogue possessed a large collection of wimpels which were kept in such order that any given wimpel was immediately available.

Ruth Eis, of the Judah L. Magnes Museum in Berkeley, California, has related an interesting incident in which the birth date of a famous rabbi could only be reliably confirmed when the binder made at his birth was discovered.

The custom in this form spread from Bavaria to the Rhineland by the end of the sixteenth century and then to Saxony and other German areas and to Bohemia and Moravia, Alsace and what is now Switzerland. By the eighteenth century it had been adopted in Holland, England and Denmark and by the late nineteenth century, the United States. It is still practised in some communities today in Switzerland and the Alsace, in Paris, London and in New York and Haifa.

Bohemia and Moravia
Jana Dolezelova has published a study of the binders in the collection of the Jewish Museum at Prague. The custom of making binders from swaddling clothes soon died out in Bohemia and Moravia, and the binders were presented on a number of different occasions. They could be in honour of a group of children, in memory of a child or a fiancé, to celebrate the foundation of a synagogue and so on.

A smaller form of binder, sometimes made of velvet, silk, wool, cotton, and occasionally leather was also produced. These measured 50 × 30 cm (19½ × 12 in.) and were tied with laces or buttons. They were far less common than the long binders.

Embroidery techniques employed on the binders included appliqué or counted thread, but the most common stitches used were stem or chain stitch.

The mappah from Italy
According to Cissy Grossman, in Italy it was customary for a woman to make and present a mappah (binder) to the synagogue on an occasion which was especially important to her. It might be when she wanted a child, or in thanksgiving at the safe birth of a baby; it could have been her wedding, or in memory of a parent. Although the formula of the embroidered dedication varied considerably it usually had some features in common: 'In honour of

diagram 45 *A dragon from an Italian binder in the Israel Museum.*

the Torah . . . this is the work of my hands . . . .
[woman's name] . . . in the year [date] . . . . .'

Fine linen or patterned silk were used to make the binder. Unlike the wimpel, the mappah, if it was pieced, was not necessarily cut from a square piece of cloth. Sometimes a binder was made to match a particular mantle.

The wimpel reflects folk embroidery, and wherever it was made, in Germany, Bohemia or Moravia, it used the folk techniques from that area. Although the mappah also reflects the life of the people, it tended to be a more subtle and sophisticated piece of embroidery. Sometimes white silk embroidery was employed on white linen, and the borders were edged with lace. There were also undyed linen binders edged with lace. The *Punto scritto* technique (double running stitch or Holbein stitch), used on contemporary domestic and ecclesiastical items, was also used in the mappot.

Modern developments in the custom of dedicating a binder

However much the customs associated with the giving of binders varied from country to country, they were usually associated with the domestic life of the community in a way which can be adapted for use today. The practice of donating binders on happy occasions and thus building up a folk history of the joyous events of a particular community is an interesting idea.

In the North Western Reform Synagogue, the custom is gaining ground and over the last few years a number of binders have been presented on the occasion of barmitzvah, batmitzvah and b'nei Torah and on the birth of grandchildren. The Jubilee of the synagogue has been commemorated in this way, and it is hoped that in time golden weddings, marriages and other happy occasions will also be marked.

Designing a Torah binder

If the binder commemorates a barmitzvah, it may well be that there is some episode in the child's portion (the part of the Torah which the boy will read aloud to the congregation) which can be used for the design.

It should be remembered that human figures were always used for Torah binders and the embroiderer can be much more free with the design here than in other items for the synagogue.

Fabric paint can be used for Torah binders, and in fact would be a continuation of the practice of painted wimpels from the nineteenth century.

It is not necessary to use a pictorial design. In the past beautifully embroidered inscriptions sometimes covered the whole length of the binder. The embroiderer can simply embroider the reason for the dedication, the date and her name in beautiful lettering. It would be more usual for the inscription to be in Hebrew. Not many of us have sufficient mastery of Hebrew to be able to write the dedication ourselves, but a rabbi or another learned Hebrew scholar should be only to happy to help. It is important to have the inscription checked by someone who is really proficient in Hebrew. I have seen a number of beautiful pieces of embroidery spoilt by having incorrect Hebrew inscriptions.

The design can be a piece of free stitchery, patchwork, or any other form of embroidery. Care must be taken that any threads which come into contact with the actual parchment of the scroll will not damage it in any way. For this reason, metal threads should be treated with caution. (*Diagram 46* shows a binder with an appliquéd chain outlined with a metal cord. The cord was omitted from the

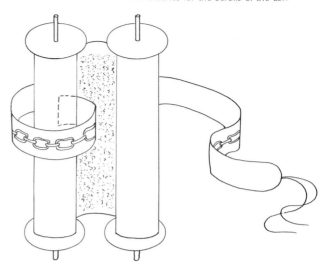

diagram 46 *The binder is tucked inside the turn of the scroll before it is wrapped around the whole scroll.*

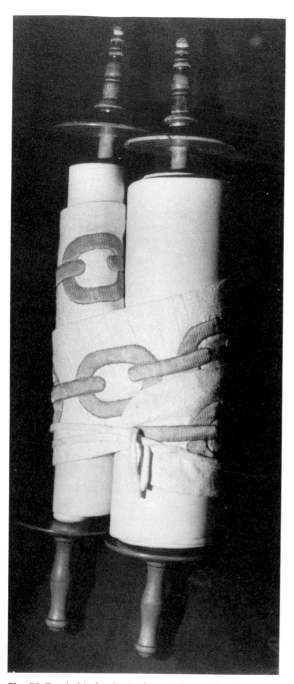

Fig. 70 *Torah binder by Kathryn Salomon for the North Western Reform Synagogue to celebrate their Golden Jubilee. Silk with fabric appliqué and metal cord.*

first two links of the chain as these would be tucked inside the scroll and any possibility of the metal touching the parchment had to be avoided.)

Making a long Torah binder

The traditional long Torah binder measures approximately 1.5 metres (1½ yards) in length and is about 18 cm (7 in.) wide. It should be long enough to enable the binder to be tucked into the turn of the scroll and to be wrapped around the scroll twice (see *diagram 46*). Ties are attached to one end for securing the binder.

The binder can be cut in one piece and folded along the top edge. This ensures that there are a minimum number of seams and that both sides of the binder are of the same quality fabric. In the past wimpels were frequently made of unlined linen.

One end of the binder is square and the other end rounded. Two cords, or possibly rouleaux of the binder material, are attached to the rounded end.

Some kind of interlining is needed. If the embroiderer wishes to have a slightly firmer binder, calico can be used. A heavyweight interlining is unsuitable as this would make the binder cumbersome to manipulate. A very lightweight interlining is quite acceptable.

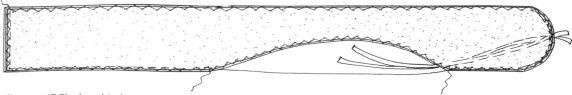

diagram 47 *The long binder, inside out, machined, but with a gap left for turning.*

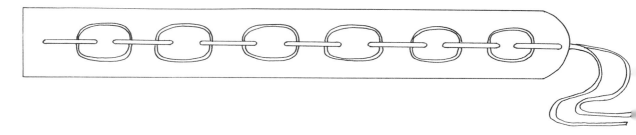

diagram 48 *The completed binder.*

The interlining is herringbone-stitched into position. Cords are attached at the rounded end and the bottom seam is machined. A gap is left to turn the binder to the right side and this is finished by hand. It is best to leave the space towards the middle of the binder. This makes the turning to the right side easier and ensures that the two ends which receive the most strain are sewn with strong machine stitching.

Making a short binder

Short binders have been used traditionally in the past and examples can be found at the Jewish Museum in Prague and elsewhere. They have always been far less common than the long binder. Short binders are popular with contemporary embroiderers as canvas work is an ideal form of embroidery for them. Other embroidery techniques can also be used. The advantage of canvas work is that the binder is then very stiff and firm; other forms of embroidery will need a stiff, belt-weight interlining.

It must be said that these short binders are much harder to use as it is difficult to ensure a really tight fit. The long binder holds the scroll more securely.

It is necessary to measure the girth of a specific scroll when making a short Torah binder. An average length for a binder is about 68 cm (26 in.) but this will vary according to the size of the scroll. The depth can be anything from 15 cm (6 in.) to 23 cm (9 in.). (Some old Italian binders are even deeper.) The binder will need to be lined with a hard-wearing lining such as cotton sateen. *Velcro* (touch-and-

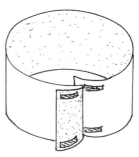

diagram 49 *The short binder, secured with velcro.*

ההרים רקדו כאילים גבעות כבני־צאן

TANYA DANIELLE GOLBY

1985   טניה דניאלה   5745

בת אשר לוי וגבריאלה

SEVENTH APRIL   SECOND DAY PESACH

Fig. 71 *Torah binder, canvas with wool embroidery, to commemorate the baby blessing of a grandchild by Helen Golby. (The North Western Reform Synagogue, London.)*

close fastener) is used today to make a quick, secure fastening. It is best to apply the *Velcro* in horizontal strips as this allows some adjustment in the binder to accommodate different scrolls.

TORAH COVERS

Orthodox communities use an embroidered cloth to cover the scroll in between the readings of different portions of the Law. (It is tradition for the scroll never to be left uncovered, so that when there is a time lapse as one person returns to their seat and another goes up to read from the Torah, the cover is placed over the scroll.)

In many synagogues today the cover is little more than a rectangular piece of fabric, usually of satin or velvet, with a dedicatory inscription embroidered upon it. The Spanish and Portuguese Jews Congregation in London possesses many fine Torah covers. It is the custom in this synagogue to have a cover which matches the parokhet, desk cover and pulpit fall. Some are decorated with floral silk embroidery on a silk ground and others use metal-thread embroidery on a velvet ground.

There is no reason why different materials cannot be used. A design does not have to match the desk cover and parokhet.

The cover should be large enough to cover the parchment of the scroll and so needs to be approximately 74 cm (29 in.) long and 40 cm (15–16 in.) wide. The cover should not be too heavy or awkward to handle as it is a functional piece. As so many contemporary Torah covers are very simple, the embroiderer is offered an opportunity to produce an original design unhampered by heavy precedent.

chapter nine

The chuppah (wedding canopy) and hangings

THE CHUPPAH

The Hebrew word *chuppah* means a canopy (Isaiah 4:5, Psalms 19:6). In biblical times the chuppah ceremony consisted of the bride being brought in festive procession to the home of her betrothed. The chuppah was either his room, or a canopy set up in his room. The Talmud refers to the father of the groom setting up the chuppah and states that it was made of precious crimson silk embroidered with gold.

The Talmud also describes the custom of the people of Bethar near Jerusalem, where a cedar tree

Fig. 72 *The wedding of Rabbi Sybil Sheridan and Rabbi Jonathan Romain. (Photo: Judy Goldhill.)*

was planted at the birth of a boy and a pine at the birth of a girl. Branches from these trees were cut down and used as the chuppah poles when a couple married (Git. 57a).

The original concept of the chuppah as the actual cohabitation of the bridal couple continued for a long time among Eastern communities, but by the Middle Ages the ceremony had become a religious one in Europe. The wedding ceremony was performed in the synagogue at first; later it took place in the courtyard outside the synagogue, where the groom formally took the bride under his protection before witnesses. As a symbol of this fact, part of his clothing, perhaps his tallit, was draped over them both. This custom also seems to be referred to in the Bible (Ruth 3:9, Ezekiel 16:8). The

earliest known representation of a wedding ceremony is to be found in a prayer book from the Rhineland (1272), and it shows the veiled bride and the groom wearing a Jew's hat standing beneath a cloth. In Israel today, and also in some communities in the Diaspora, a wedding is sometimes solemnized beneath a tallit, either held up or fixed to four poles. This custom may well have developed from the ancient practice mentioned above. The concept of the chuppah as a tallit can be developed by the embroiderer and will be discussed in more detail later.

It seems that the wedding ceremony as we know it today was considered a recent innovation in the sixteenth century, because it is described as such by Moses Isserles. If we as embroiderers and designers consider the different antecedents to the modern chuppah, we can make good use of them to produce exciting modern designs.

Fig. 73 *Chuppah, worked with blessings from the marriage service in gold kid outlined with pearl purl, by Louis Grossé Ltd. for the Spanish and Portuguese Jews Congregation, London.*

Different approaches to designing a chuppah

A personal chuppah
A family can commission or make a chuppah for the personal use of that particular family through the generations. It can be designed in such a way that it can become a hanging when not in use for a wedding ceremony.

A tallit/chuppah
A bride can commission or make a beautiful tallit which will be used as the chuppah for her wedding and become the tallit her husband will wear after they are married. In Polish Sephardi communities in the past men did not wear a tallit until they were married, and in some communities a tallit was given to the groom by the bride on the occasion of their wedding.

Fig. 74 *Chuppah by Ita Aber.*

Fig. 75 *Chuppah by Temma Gentles; hand-painted silk appliquéd on to polyester. A text from the marriage blessings is painted on the streamers. 385 × 305 × 365 cm (13 × 10 × 12 ft). (Holy Blossom Temple, Toronto.)*

Fig. 76 *Chuppah, by Temma Gentles; polyester, silk, cotton cord. Each side of the triangles measures 550 cm (18 ft). (Temple Emanú-El, Toronto.)*

The chuppah as a hanging for the synagogue

The synagogue chuppah can also be designed so that it can be used as a hanging when it is not needed for a wedding ceremony. It can either take the form of a conventional wall hanging, or it can be suspended from the ceiling of the synagogue, lowered for the wedding ceremony, and raised when not in use.

If a chuppah is designed in this way, not only will the congregation be able to appreciate its beauty throughout the year, but the chuppah will benefit from not being folded up in a box between weddings. Storing a chuppah is a problem, and this method solves the difficulty and allows the chuppah to be appreciated by many people.

The chuppah as a room

As has been described, the chuppah was originally the bridegroom's chamber and the idea of the chuppah as a room has been explored by a number of designers.

An Israeli artist, Yaakov Boussidan, has designed a large hanging which is hung in the room where a wedding takes place. The wedding ceremony does not have to take place in a synagogue at all. Many synagogues possess travelling chuppot for use in other places. The wedding can be solemnized in a private home, in the open air, or at the place where the wedding reception will be held.

In Chapter 11 I touched upon nineteenth-century experiments in synagogue architecture. The Hampstead Synagogue, London reflects an oriental

diagram 50 *The chuppah from the New West End Synagogue, London.*

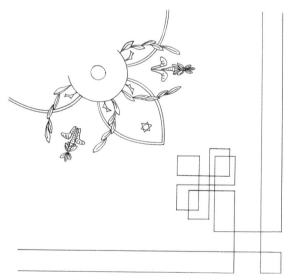

diagram 51 *The ceiling of the chuppah from the New West End Synagogue.*

Fig. 77 *Chuppah, by Ina Golub; appliquéd Indian silk on linen. 'You are my beloved and I am yours' from the Song of Songs. 185 × 185 × 180 cm (6 ft 2 in. × 6 ft 2 in. × 6 ft). (Collection of Mr and Mrs Richard Janger.)*

influence and there are a number of small domes in the roof. The chuppah has been designed to complement the architecture and is in the form of a dome. It can thus be seen that contrary to general belief Orthodox synagogues in Britain are prepared to consider original designs, and the embroiderer should take heart and be more ambitious in the choice of design for synagogue items.

Embroiderers in the United States have explored the concept of the chuppah as a room in a different manner. One side of the chuppah is lengthened to become a 'wall' of embroidery. The wedding is solemnized with the bridal pair facing the rabbi, who stands with his back to the embroidery.

Areas of the chuppah to be considered for embroidery

The areas most usually embroidered on the chuppah are the four pelmet-like panels which hang down on all four sides. The most favoured form of embroidery consists of quotations from the blessings which form part of the wedding ceremony. (A commonly used format is given below.)

There are chuppot from earlier times which have not only the side panels embroidered, but also the ceiling of the chuppah. If the wedding party look up, they will see the embroidery. As some chuppot have bars across the ceiling area to stop the roof sagging, the designer will have to examine the method each synagogue uses to support the chuppah before considering which areas to embroider.

Phrases from the seven benedictions which are recited at the wedding service are frequently found on the side panels of contemporary chuppot. The phrases are often embroidered one on each panel:

1 The voice of joy   קול ששון

2 and the voice of gladness   וקל שמחה

3 the voice of the bridegroom   קול חתן

4 and the voice of the bride   וקול כלה

Fig. 78 *Detail of chuppah for South West Essex Reform Synagogue, London, by Pauline Brown. Appliquéd silk with embroidery in metallic and cotton threads and beads.*

Symbolism which can be used to decorate the chuppah

Many chuppot contain little more decoration than the phrases given above. However, there are symbols which have been used in the past, usually referring to fertility.

In Germany in the sixteenth century a chuppah was sometimes made of blue fabric and the sun, moon and stars were embroidered upon it to represent the sky. They were intended as an omen, 'that their children shall be as numerous as the stars of heaven' (God's promise to Abraham, Genesis 15:5). A chuppah with decoration which represents the sky would also recall the time when most wedding ceremonies were performed in the open air.

The pomegranate is an ancient fertility symbol which is also very attractive. The embroiderer can explore ideas from the Song of Songs which would be most appropriate.

As the chuppah is usually decorated with flowers, the floral decoration can be carried over into the design for the chuppah.

Colours and fabrics for a chuppah

The chuppah can be made of any material or colour which the synagogue, the congregation and the designer desire. Many contemporary chuppot are made of red or blue velvet, or white silk or satin, but there is no special reason for this. (White is, of course, always symbolic for a wedding.)

Using flowers to decorate a chuppah

A chuppah is usually decorated with flowers for the wedding ceremony. It may be that only the four poles are decorated (as in *fig. 73*); however, sometimes the florist pins the flowers to the four sides of the chuppah itself. For this reason it would be unwise to use very elaborate or delicate embroidery. It would be heartbreaking to spend many hours producing a work of art and then find that it had been ruined by the florists who decorate the chuppah. It may be that a congregation would wish to have a very special chuppah and so forbid the pinning of flowers to the embroidery. This would have to be considered and discussed in advance.

Making a chuppah

An average chuppah is about 188 cm (6 ft 2 in.) square. The depth of the four sides would have to be in proportion: 42 cm (16 in.), without a fringe, is an indication.

A chuppah must be made of a hard-wearing furnishing fabric which does not crease easily. The lining needs to be considered with care as it will always be visible when the chuppah is in use. Some chuppot are lined with sateen, and this is the most durable and practical lining fabric. It is not necessarily the most aesthetically pleasing. The embroiderer will have to consider whether she wishes the interior of the chuppah to be an area which attracts attention or not.

The tendency of the chuppah to sag can be a problem. Some chuppot have a hole in the centre for a light and this means that there is less fabric to

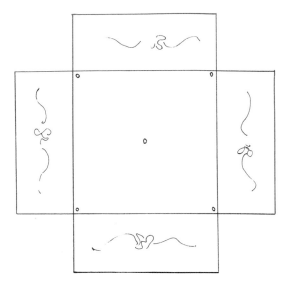

diagram 52 *Plan of a chuppah.*

sag. Some chuppot frames are constructed with crossbars to hold the chuppah posts firm and this will counteract any sagging. Others are mounted over a hard frame. The actual method of supporting a chuppah used by different synagogues will have to be investigated before the embroiderer can begin to design.

Every chuppah will have a hole in each of the four corners of the top piece where the chuppah poles will pass through the fabric. There may also be a central hole through which a light is suspended. These holes will need reinforcement, either by leather in a colour matching the lining, or by metal eyelets (which can be obtained from a yacht chandler's).

1 The top and the four sides of the chuppah are cut out, making sure that the grain of the fabric runs in the same direction on all the pieces.

2 The sections of the top piece are tacked, machined and the seams pressed open.

3 The interlining is cut out. If pieces need to be joined they are sewn together with an overlapping seam and with a zigzag stitch. The seam should run in the same direction as the seams on the top fabric. The interlining is 'locked' to the top fabric and the edges are tacked and herringbone-stitched into position.

4 The lining is cut out, with the grain running in the same direction as the top fabric. (In both cases the selvedge should run the length of the chuppah, and be cut off.) The seams are machined, and pressed open. The lining is placed upon the interlining with the seams facing inward, and is 'locked' into position. The top of the chuppah is tacked all the way round.

5 The holes for the chuppah poles are made, and reinforced either by metal eyelets or by a circle of leather applied to the underside of the chuppah.

6 The interlining is cut out and 'locked' on to the fabric of the side pieces. It is tacked and herringbone-stitched into position. The lining is 'locked' to the interlining and tacked.

7 The side pieces are finished off on three sides, leaving the top for the moment. Corners will need to be mitred.

8 The tacking is removed from the top piece of the chuppah and the side pieces are tacked and stitched to the top piece. When all four side pieces have been attached, the lining of the top piece is drawn over the raw edges and sewn to give a neat finish.

9 Hooks and eyes can be sewn on to the edges of the four side panels if desired, to close the corners. If the poles of the chuppah are attractive there is no reason why the four panels cannot hang loose. The reason the corners are closed with hooks and eyes rather than being sewn together, is so that the chuppah can be folded away without making extra creases in the side pieces.

HANGINGS

Hangings were of great importance in the Sanctuary in the desert. They were used to separate areas of greater and lesser holiness (Exodus 26:33). The varying degrees of holiness were symbolized by the use of different colours. The actual Sanctuary was made with curtains of 'fine twined linen, and blue and purple and scarlet, with cherubim, the work of the skilful workman worked into them'. A screen was made for the doorway of the Tent, in the same materials. The courtyard of the Tabernacle was enclosed within hangings of linen. The modern embroiderer can point to the importance of hangings for the Sanctuary in ancient times when producing panels for synagogues today.

Fig. 79 *One of a pair of hangings made of canvas work by some 40 members of the congregation of the North Western Reform Synagogue under the direction of Jane Stevens, based on designs by Shraga Weil. 'A time to keep' (this hanging) and 'A time to cast away'. (230 × 150 cm (7 ft 6 in. × 4 ft 11 in.)*

Fig. 80 *Members of the North Western Reform Synagogue working upon the hangings.*

The Yeshurun Synagogue, Manchester, has introduced colour and warmth into its prayer hall by the use of hangings rather than the more conventional stained glass windows. Beryl Patten and Judy Barry were commissioned to produce 12 hangings on the theme of the Twelve Tribes. A carefully planned colour scheme follows the colours of the spectrum through reds and blues around the synagogue walls.

Other synagogues have commissioned professional embroiderers to design hangings which members of the community have worked under their supervision. The sisterhood of the Beth El Temple in Ohio have produced not only the canvas work Ark doors in figure 55 but also a series of panels. The women of the North Western Reform Synagogue, London, produced two hangings based on designs by Shraga Weil under the direction of Jane Stevens.

Communal projects enrich the synagogue building and build links within the community. Care needs to be taken in choosing not only the design but also the person who will lead the group, as a project by a religious community can have special problems. It can be hard to maintain a high standard of workmanship, as this may mean turning away willing helpers whose technical skills are not up to standard. The leader needs great patience and tact. However, communal projects are both ambitious and exciting and the rewards are very great.

chapter ten

Jewish ceremonial embroideries for domestic and personal use and festivals

As many Jewish religious ceremonies are carried out in the home, there is a rich heritage of both professionally made items and folk art. There are also many embroidered items for personal use.

When I first started to embroider I thought that people were far more adept at designing embroideries in the past and that it was only the advent of the Industrial Revolution and commercial kits which had made some embroiderers afraid of producing their own designs. Of course I soon found out that although there was a great deterioration in design in the late nineteenth and early twentieth centuries, embroiderers have always either adapted designs from other sources or commissioned artists to produce designs for them. However, my original idea is a beautiful fantasy and is borne out by the wonderful heritage of Jewish folk art. Does it matter if the designs do not have classical proportions? The items produced were rich and varied, and they are as true a history of the Jewish people as the professionally produced pieces. Both have their place, both are important. Of course domestic items have always been made both to a high professional standard and in a more naïve style. It is very sad that so many people today buy inferior, mass-produced pieces rather than attempting to make their own family heirlooms.

THE TALLIT

Jewish men wear a *tallit* or prayer shawl for morning and additional prayers. There are occasions when the tallit is also worn for afternoon or evening prayers, or all day, such as on the Day of Atonement. Slightly different rules from those which affect the ordinary congregant govern the occasions on which the reader or *chazan* wears a tallit.

The commandment to wear a prayer shawl comes from Numbers 15:37–9. In biblical times the tallit was a woollen outer garment worn by men, similar to the *abbayah* worn by the Bedouin today. The influence of Hellenism upon the dress of Jews was considerable and can be seen in the frescoes from the Dura Europos Synagogue in which people are portrayed in full Greek dress. At that time a different type of tallit developed, similar to the robe worn by Greek and Roman philosophers and poets. It may well be that there are also influences upon the tallit of a robe worn for pagan religious ceremonies. After the exile the tallit was no longer worn as the outer garment, but became an item worn specifically for prayer.

Colour of the tallit

The tallit is usually white. White has always been a symbol of purity (Psalms 104:2). The Essenes (a sect active in Judah at the end of the Second Temple period) gave a white robe to each new member on his acceptance into the Order.

The stripes

The custom of putting stripes and fringes upon the garments of scribes in Palestine was noted by Epiphanius, who refers to purple stripes. It is probable that the blue colour with which the stripes and the thread of blue were dyed in ancient times was in fact the famous purple obtained from a shellfish. In any event, when the specific colour became unobtainable, the rabbis decided that any imitation was inferior and abandoned the blue stripe.

When looking at tallitot in museums, one can see white as well as black stripes. Today, the most common colours in Britain are blue or black.

In the United States many brightly coloured tallitot are worn. Some have multi-coloured stripes.

Size and shape

Rabbinic instructions state that the length of the tallit should be a hand-breadth shorter than the garment worn beneath it (BB 57b). This custom is not necessarily adhered to today, and one sees tallitot of varying widths and lengths.

In the United States very narrow tallitot are sometimes worn, but it would be very unusual to see such a narrow tallit in Britain.

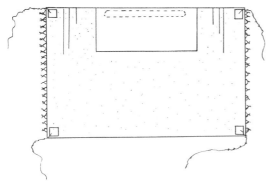

diagram 53 *A large tallit measuring 175 × 125 cm (69 × 49 in.) The reinforced area over the shoulders measure 38 × 45 cm (15 × 18 in.). Note the position of the atarah which would be appliqued to the right side of the tallit, and the reinforced corners.*

Fig. 81 *Tallit by Pat Russell; white wool with embroidered lettering in gold with touches of colour. (Photo: Ian Ross.)*

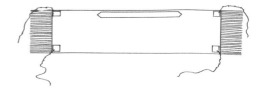

diagram 54 *A narrow tallit measuring 175 × 65 cm (69 × 25 in.). The position of the atarah and tzitzit are shown.*

The tallit is essentially a square or rectangular piece of fabric with long fringes in the four corners. Here again there are differences between Britain and the United States. The tallit most commonly worn in the United Kingdom is the rectangular or square shape referred to above. In America or Canada very narrow tallitot are worn in Progressive synagogues. Sometimes they are made with a shaped neckline, or with darts so that the tallit drapes well around the neck of the wearer. This would be most unusual in Britain.

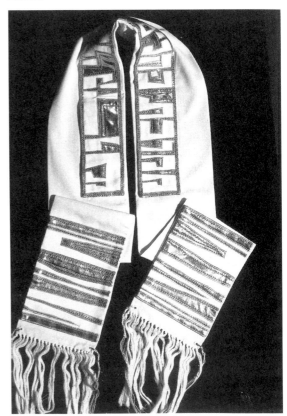

Different customs and styles in different countries in the past

A visit to a Jewish museum will show that tallitot varied from country to country in the past. Italian Jews have worn tallitot profusely decorated with beautiful embroidery. A distinctive form of embroidery was used for the *atarah* (literally 'crown', the neckband of the tallit) from Poland. Yemenite Jews developed very distinctive and colourful tallitot.

There are also different customs attached to the occasion when a Jew commenced wearing a tallit. In Polish Sephardi communities the tallit was worn by the married men. It was often a gift from the bride to the bridegroom. In Oriental communities the tallit is worn by unmarried men and in Sephardi and Ashkenazi communities it is worn by children.

There are Liberal synagogues where only the rabbi, the reader, and those called to the Reading of the Law wear a tallit, and others where some men wear them and others do not. With the advent of the Women's Liberation Movement, there has been a move for women to wear tallitot in Progressive synagogues. It is not a common practice in Britain, but one can see a time when special tallitot designed for women will become popular.

Fabric for a tallit

It is not necessary to have stripes on a tallit, so any suitable fabric can be chosen and the ends fringed and possibly knotted, with tzitzit attached to the four corners.

The fabric should be pleasant to wear. It should be reasonably light, for coolness in summer, and needs to be crease-resistant. A very slippery material would need constant rearrangement and so be rather irritating for the wearer. The larger tallitot are worn with the sides folded back upon themselves exposing the underside of the garment. This must be considered when choosing both the fabric and the method of embroidery.

Embroidery for the tallit

Beautiful antique tallitot can be seen in museums, with large areas of embroidery. One particular example in the Israel Museum is lavishly decorated

diagram 55 *Narrow tallit.*

115

with flowers and peacocks. A tallit embroidered in this way would be unusual today; the average British male is very conservative and would not wear it. However, perhaps this is a model which could be considered for an essentially feminine tallit. There are specific areas of the tallit which lend themselves to embroidery, and which are, perhaps, more acceptable to masculine taste:

The stripes

Although it is not necessary to have stripes, it is traditional and it is possible to create embroidered ones, or to use fabric paint to paint them. A combination of the two techniques is also a possibility. The stripes can be made by fabric appliqué or by stitchery (hand or machine). The use of cords and fine ribbons can also be explored. An

embroidered tallit will almost certainly need to be lined. This is not usual today, but there is no reason why it should not be done.

The atarah

The atarah is usually embroidered separately and attached to the tallit.

In the past large square pieces of especially beautiful fabric have been used, as well as the long narrow shape customary today. A very special method of decorating the atarah was developed in Russia and Poland in the nineteenth and early twentieth centuries. It is known as 'Spanier arbeit' (Spanish work) and seems to have been produced by winding silver or gold threads around a cotton core, by means of a wooden frame. Spanier work was used for atarot, kippot and some other items worn specifically by Jewish brides in the past.

Fig. 82 *Tallit by Joan Koslan Schwarz; appliqué and surface embroidery, 138 × 220 cm (4 ft 6 × 7 ft 2 in.)*

Fig. 83 *Ornament for a tallit, Germany. (Israel Museum, Jerusalem.)*

Fig. 84 *Tallit; French, first quarter of the eighteenth century, silk on silk, long and short satin and stem stitch with French knots and laid and couched work. (Victoria & Albert Museum, London.)*

Fig. 85 *White silk tallit; French, mid-eighteenth century. Panel of brocaded silk enriched with metal thread and a pattern of ribbons and brocade flowers. The top border has heavy metal-thread embroidery. The appliquéd corners match the atarah. (Jewish Museum, London.)*

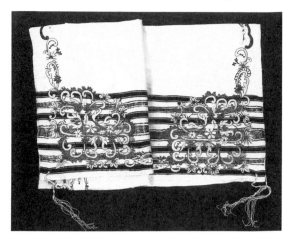

Fig. 87 *Tallit; Livorno, Italy, second half of the nineteenth century, gold thread embroidery. (Israel Museum, Jerusalem.)*

Fig. 86 *A personalized atarah in canvas work by Leni Taussig for Rabbi Wilfred Solomon. The six symbols are translations of the Hebrew names of each member of the family.*

Embroidered corners

Examples of embroidered corners for the tallit can be found in museums and amongst Sephardi Jews today. I have not been able to ascertain whether this is a specifically Sephardi practice, but it is certainly one which Jews from other backgrounds could consider. Figure *87* shows two complete corners of a tallit which have been embroidered. Examples of detachable embroidered corners can also be found in museums. Figure *85* shows corners which have been made to match the atarah and appliquéd to the tallit. The atarah and the corners could be embroidered as a set and given as a gift on the occasion of a wedding or a special anniversary.

The tzitzit

Long threads are threaded through the four corners of the tallit and knotted in a special way. (The threads are best bought from a shop which specializes in Judaica, but can be made to match the tallit.) Different methods of knotting and winding the threads are used by Ashkenazi and Sephardi Jews. Very precise details for tying the tzitzit can be found in the *First Jewish Catalog*, by Richard Segal, Michael and Sharon Strassfeld. More general details are given in diagrams *56*, *57* and *58*.

Any method of embroidery can be used for the atarah. Obviously cleaning must be considered. Either it must be possible to remove the atarah when the tallit is laundered or the atarah must be washable.

There are a number of phrases which lend themselves to being embroidered upon a tallit; for example, part of the blessing for putting on the tallit, or a suitable quotation from the Bible. Flowers, abstract designs and patterns can all be used.

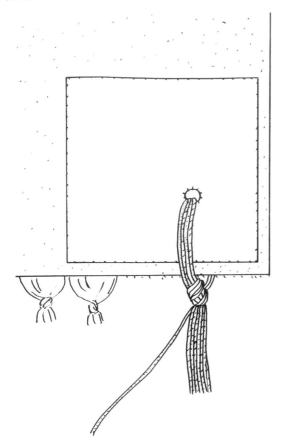

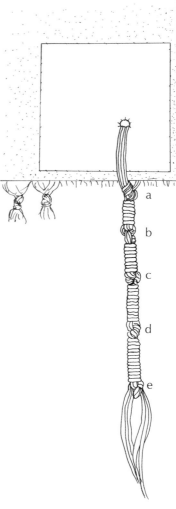

diagram 56 *Eight threads are used for each corner. The tzitzit is commenced with a double knot, and then one thread, which is much longer than the other seven, is wound around the other threads.*

diagram 57 *The completed tzitzit. By the time the correct number of coils and knots has been made, a fairly long fringe of equal length threads will be left. (a) double knot; (b) 7 coils and double knot; (c) 8 coils and double knot; (d) 11 coils and double knot; (e) 13 coils and double knot.*

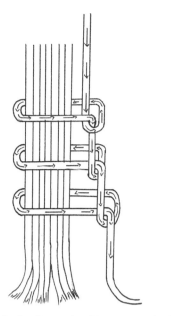

diagram 58 *The Sephardi way of making tzitzit with a knot in between each coil.*

TALLIT BAGS

It is customary to keep a tallit in a special bag. Phylacteries are also kept in a bag and sometimes these have been made to match the tallit bag.

The commercially made bags available in Britain are usually red or blue velvet. People automatically think of velvet in the above colours when choosing the fabric, but a tallit bag can be of any colour and material which the embroiderer and the user can agree. Remnants of handwoven tweeds or unusual fabrics can make excellent bags. Canvas work embroidery lends itself to the purpose admirably.

Size

The bag should be large enough to hold the tallit without it being folded over too many times and so becoming creased. Some men keep their prayer book in the bag, and this would increase the size.

Fig. 88 *Tallit bag; Yemenite embroidery upon velvet, cotton and metal threads.* (Property of Raymond Goldman.)

Fig. 89 *Tallit bag; Jerusalem, 1880. (Israel Museum, Jerusalem.)*

Fig. 90 *Tallit bag by Diane Langleben, London, on the theme of peoples of the world. Natural raw silk with laid work, couching and chain stitch in cotton and metallic threads in shades of brown.*

Matching tallit bag and kippah

Tallit bags and kippot are sometimes made to match as a gift for a specific occasion.

Symbolism

Symbols relevant to the Sabbath or festivals can be used, as can flowers, fruit or abstract decoration. I would make a plea for the avoidance of the Star of David, which has become such an overworked emblem. Lettering, the word *tallit* (in Hebrew) for example, or the owner's name or initials can be sufficient decoration in themselves.

Making a tallit bag

The bag and the lining are cut exactly the same size. The material is folded so that a seam on each side creates a bag. Press seams and turn to right side. The raw edges are turned in at the top edge and a zip is tacked and then sewn in. The lining is slipped in, wrong side out, and attached to the bag. If a very bulky fabric is used, it may be better to turn the top edges down and hem them to the lining. A strip of lining material, cut on the bias, can then be used to cover the raw edge and so give a neat finish.

Another method of making a bag is to cut the fabric in one piece with an extra allowance for a flap. Two-thirds of the material are folded and stitched and become the bag. The remaining third is the flap.

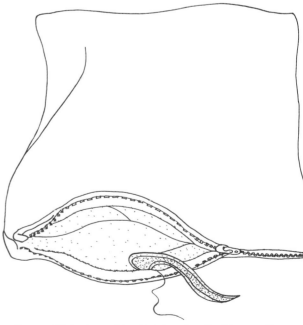

diagram 59 *Sewing a strip of fabric cut on the bias over the raw edge inside the tallit bag.*

The lining is made in exactly the same way and is slipped into the bag, with all the seams inwards. The lining is stitched by hand to the flap and around the top edge of the bag. Buttons and loops are used to secure the flap.

THE KIPPAH (SKULL CAP)

Exodus 28:4, 37, 39, 40, refer to the mitre worn by the High Priest and the hats worn by the other priests, but it seems that in biblical times the general population did not cover their heads for prayer. At that time the covering of the head was a mark of religious status. After the destruction of the Temple, Rabbis and lay members of the congregation replaced the Priests as leaders of the community and

Fig. 92 *Kippah from Israel; Bokharan work, canvas work embroidery.* (Property of Douglas Blackman.)

Fig. 91 *Velvet smoking cap with silk embroidery, nineteenth century.* (Property of the Ziege family, who use it as a kippah.)

Fig. 93 *Kippah by Esther Carvalho, London; silk and metal-thread embroidery and sequins on reversed satin.* (Property of Mr R. N. Carvalho.)

Fig. 94 *Kippah, possibly from Turkestan or Bokhara; canvas-work embroidery. (Property of Jonathan Epstein.)*

they too adopted the custom, long before it was adopted by the whole congregation. Wearing a hat to denote status is a universal custom. Today, in some communities in Britain, the wardens of the synagogue wear top hats as opposed to the *kippot* or ordinary hats worn by the rest of the men.

It seems that the concept of covering the head for prayer is probably an Eastern custom adopted by the Babylonian exiles from their neighbours and spread by them to the different countries in which they later settled. The Talmud (Ned 30b) refers to the practice of covering the head for prayer as a custom but not an obligation, and so it remained for a long time. A French rabbi expressed surprise at seeing the head

covered for prayer in a Spanish synagogue in the twelfth century. Moses Isserles, a sixteenth-century commentator, felt it was good manners to cover the head, but not obligatory. During this century in German communities, boys were called to the Reading of the Law bare-headed.

It seems probable that the custom spread because of the Jews' wish to differentiate themselves from Christians, in much the same way that early Christians deliberately went bare-headed to differentiate themselves from Jews. David Ostrog, who lived in the seventeenth century, gives this reason for wearing hats for prayer.

From the Middle Ages onwards Jews in different parts of Europe were forced to wear special clothes and hats to set them apart. In later times Jews have deliberately chosen to wear the kippah as a badge of Jewishness, as can be seen in contemporary Jewish

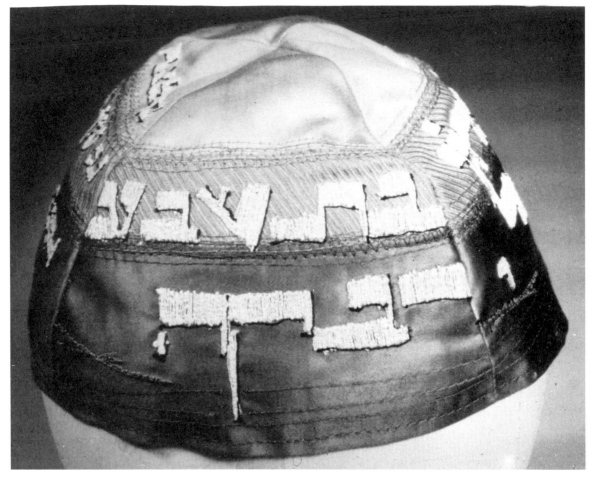

Fig. 95 *Kippah by Joan Koslan-Swartz: appliqué under machine embroidery.*

communities. The current expression of pride shown by many ethnic groups is shared by Jews and the wearing of some obvious identification, even in the street, is the result.

There are some Liberal Jews who choose to pray with their heads uncovered as they feel this is the most authentic custom.

Materials for a kippah

The only constraints upon the design and material for a kippah are the suitability of the fabric and the disposition of the wearer. The men in my family tend to prefer the simplest and plainest of designs, but happily for the embroiderer not all men agree with them and many can be seen displaying unusual multi-coloured kippot in our synagogues. Some men collect kippot from different countries, and some wear the hand-embroidered hats which are made by the Druze in Israel. These are not kippot, but are sufficiently similar to be worn and to be of interest to the embroiderer.

Kippot for special occasions

A special kippah can be made for a specific festival – a barmitzvah, a wedding, or to celebrate an honour given by the community. When a member of the North Western Reform Synagogue was chosen to be the Bridegroom of the Law at the festival of Simchat Torah (Rejoicing of the Law) his wife made a special kippah to commemorate the event.

Making a kippah

Diagram 60 shows one quarter of a kippah which can be enlarged and used as a pattern.

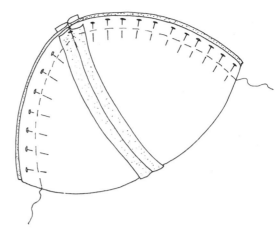

diagram 62 *Two quarters are sewn together, and then the two halves are joined.*

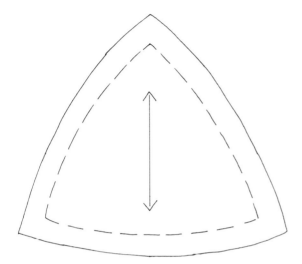

diagram 60 *One quarter of a kippah.*

The four quarters of the kippah are cut out with the grain of the fabric running in the same direction in each section through the centre of each piece.

The kippah is embroidered before it is assembled. If there is to be a continuous design over all the sections, the design is stopped a little distance from the seam allowance and finished after the kippah has been assembled.

Two quarters are sewn together, then the two halves are joined. Care must be taken to ensure that all the centre points meet. The lining is made in the same way, placed inside the kippah and hemmed to it.

diagram 63 *The lining is placed inside the kippah and attached to it.*

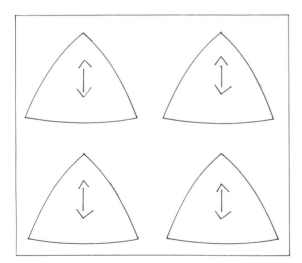

diagram 61 *The four quarters of the kippah are cut out with the grain of the fabric running in the same direction in each section, through the centre of each piece.*

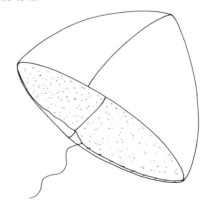

127

chapter eleven

Embroideries for the Sabbath and festivals

Traditionally the table is always laid with a fine white cloth for the Sabbath and for festivals, and the best china and cutlery are used. In times of great poverty families struggled to provide special treats for the Sabbath meal, even if they went hungry for the rest of the week, and they laid the Sabbath or festive table in the best manner possible.

In the past, special tablecentres or tablecloths were produced for the Sabbath or for festivals. Often they contained appropriate biblical quotations, and symbolic illustrations and decorations. In Jerusalem, during the nineteenth century, Simche Januver drew designs on tablecloths especially for people to embroider. Examples of his designs can be found in the Israel Museum, the Jewish Museum, London, and the Victoria and Albert Museum, London.

Special tablecentres or tablecloths can be made for specific Jewish festivals and embroidered with symbols appropriate to that festival. (See embroideries for the Seder table, page 133.)

Fabric paint can be used in conjunction with embroidery. Methods to be considered are freehand painting, or block or screen printing. The paint can then be enriched and embellished with embroidery to produce a satisfying result.

Fig. 96 *Challah cover by Kathryn Salomon; cotton and metallic thread surface embroidery upon linen.*

Fig. 97 *Challah cover by Marianna Kirchstein; silk with silk and wool embroidery. (Hebrew Union College Skirball Museum, Los Angeles.)*

THE CHALLAH CLOTH

On the eve of the Sabbath and festivals, the Sabbath (or festive) candles are lit just before sunset. The family recites the 'Kiddush' which consists of some prayers and a sip of wine. After the Kiddush, the grace before meals is said over special plaited bread, known as *challah*, which is always used for Shabbat and festivals. The challot are covered with a challah cloth during the Kiddush.

Early challah cloths may have been little more than a napkin placed over the bread, but in later times they became more elaborate.

Symbolism for a challah cloth

The challah itself has always been used in design; the rounded form of the plaited bread, and the rich colours can produce interesting shapes and textures. Figure 98 shows a challah cloth worked in Assisi work with the subject left void and the background covered with cross stitch.

As shown in figures 98 and 99, the Shabbat candles are often used as symbols, either in conjunction with the challah, or by themselves. The actual blessing for the bread has also been used to decorate challah cloths as in figure 96.

Fig. 98 *Challah cover by Gillian Epstein for the Alyth Kindergarten, London. Red cotton upon a white ground, Assisi work.*

diagram 64 *Design for a challah cloth.*

Fig. 99 *Challah cover by Naomi Cohen-Ziv, London; cotton
and satin, machine embroidery.*

Fig. 100 *Challah cover by Sharon Norry, Rochester, New York; cotton and metallic thread embroidery, backstitch upon a handwoven linen ground.*

For a more unusual approach to symbolism, one could consider the idea that every Sabbath we recall the creation of the world and that the Sabbath celebrates the completion of creation.

Challah cloths are used for festivals as well as Shabbat and special challah cloths with the appropriate symbolism for a specific festival can be made.

Passover, the festival which commemorates the Exodus from Egypt, is celebrated by a service in the home, followed by a meal and communal singing. It is called the Seder (which literally means 'Order', as in order of service).

The table is set with beautiful items kept especially for the occasion. Many symbolic rituals

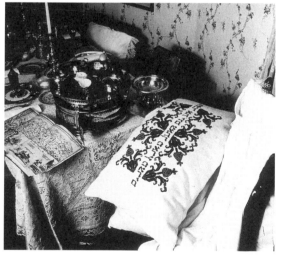

Fig. 101 *Passover pillowcase, embroidered on white linen by Gladys Rosen and lent by her for the Traditional Seder from The Art of Celebration Exhibition at the Yeshiva University Museum, New York, 1984–86. Note the antique silver seder plate. On the top are the symbolic foods used during the seder service and the doors are open to reveal three pieces of matzot.*

133

are performed during the evening and some of these rituals need items which can be embroidered.

TABLECLOTHS AND BANNERS

Recently, I met a family who own a special cloth which was embroidered by a relation in nineteenth-century Germany and which was made specifically to adorn the Seder table. They also use a banner, embroidered by the same person, which they hang up in the dining-room during the festival of Passover.

The embroiderer has worked a representation of the four types of Jew who attend the Seder Service, as portrayed in the haggadah by the four sons: one wise, one wicked, one simple, and one who is too

Fig. 102 *Passover banner by Ella Schwab; linen, turn of the century. (Property of Mr Simons.)*

young to ask questions. The design she has chosen has been taken from an illustration in a sixteenth-century haggadah, which was copied in many later haggadot; it depicts the wicked son as a soldier.

THE MATZAH CLOTH

Unleavened bread, or *matzah*, is eaten during the eight days of Passover, and three pieces are kept in a special bag known as a matzah cloth. They are used symbolically during the Seder service. The bag has three compartments for the three pieces of matzah. Silver dishes were sometimes used in the past (*fig. 101*). There are still occasional examples of silver boxes today. Sometimes they consist of three trays one above the other, with a curtain, possibly embroidered, which could be drawn to conceal the matzah, and opened to disclose it at the appropriate place in the Seder service.

Size, shape and materials for a matzah cloth

In the past matzah cloths were made from velvet and silk, and they were elaborately embroidered with silk and metal threads. The use of fish scales in

Fig. 103 *Matzah cloth; silk with silk embroidery and beads and a metallic fringe. Dated 1900. 56 cm (22 in.) including fringe. (Private collection.)*

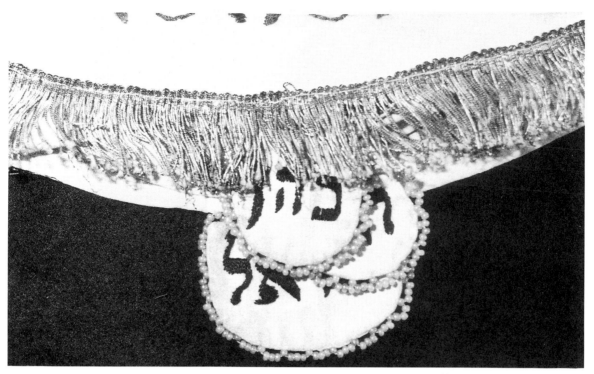

Fig. 104 *Detail of fig. 108, showing embroidered tags for each of the three pockets. The top pocket is labelled Cohanim (Priests), the second layer Levites (the Priestly servants in the Temple) and the bottom layer is labelled Israel for the people.*

embroidery, which became popular in Victorian times, can be seen on some nineteenth-century cloths.

The silk and velvet cloths with metal-thread embroidery would have been impossible to clean. It is possible to make a cloth with metal thread embroidery, and to have a detachable bag beneath it for the three pieces of matzah. One must bear in mind that the cloth is only used once a year, so cleaning is not a major problem. Linen, of course, is ideal.

Many antique cloths were round, perhaps indicating that the matzot were round too. As contemporary matzot are often square there is no reason why a square cloth should not be made.

The modern family dining-room and dining table are much smaller than in former times, and so it is impractical to make a large cloth as it will take up too much room on the Seder table. An average size for a matzah cloth is 37 cm (14 in.) but the embroiderer should make the size suitable for her needs.

Matzah cloths for the communal Seder
Many synagogues today hold communal Seder services and so need a large number of matzah cloths for all the families who participate. The Guild of the North Western Reform Synagogue produced a large quantity of identical matzah cloths especially for use at the communal Seder. This is a project which is relatively easy for a group to undertake. The design is chosen, the fabrics and embroidery threads purchased and the stitches decided. The individual members are then delegated to make a matzah cloth each. It would be a good idea to include the date the project was undertaken somewhere on each cloth as this would be of historical interest in the future.

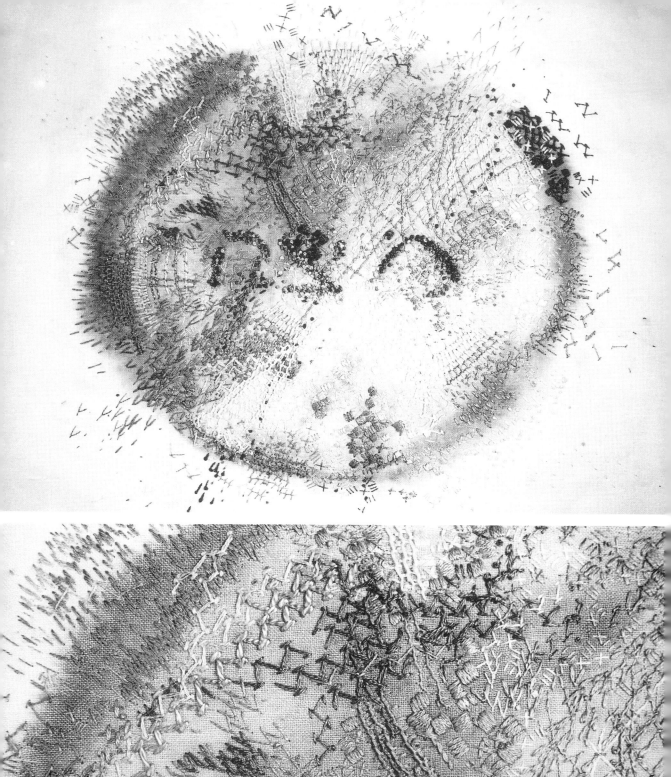
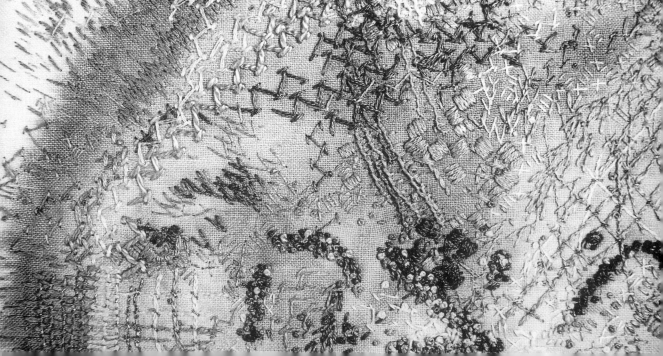

Symbolism for a matzah cloth

Many matzah cloths are embroidered with a design of the Seder plate. This is the dish which contains a number of symbolic objects, some of which are eaten or dipped into other substances, others of which are alluded to for symbolic reasons at different points in the Seder service.

Some cloths contain the word 'matzah' or 'Pesach' (Passover). As Passover is a spring festival, spring flowers and lambs are appropriate. (The Pascal lamb, the offering which was made at the Temple, is represented upon the Seder dish by a roasted bone.)

Making a matzah cloth

A simple way to make a matzah cloth is to have four pieces of linen of equal size which are placed one on top of the other. The individual pieces are first hemmed and the top piece is embroidered with an appropriate design. The four corners of all the pieces are caught together. Tassles can be made of the embroidery threads used for the stitchery and attached to the corners.

diagram 66 *Three pieces of material are machined together to form a bag. The sides are trimmed and then the bag is turned and pressed.*

diagram 65 *Making a matzah cloth by catching the 4 layers of fabric at the corners.*

Alternatively, a bag can be made of the bottom two pockets, machined and turned and pressed so that the raw edges are inside. The top layer can be attached separately (having previously been hemmed).

Lace or another form of decorative border can be used around the top edge. Many commercially made matzah cloths have a fringe around them to conceal the raw edges. It is usually far too heavy, and should not be copied; with a little thought a far more suitable method of finishing can be devised.

diagram 67 *The top pocket is made by attaching the embroidery to the top layer of the bag.*

Fig. 105 *Matzah cloth by Kathryn Salomon. Fabric paint and stitchery in cotton and metallic thread upon a linen ground. The layers are caught together at the four corners and the tassles are made of the embroidery threads.*

Fig. 106 *Detail of fig. 105.*

Fig. 107 *Passover pillowcase; linen embroidery upon linen.*
(Hebrew Union College Skirball Museum, Los Angeles.)

PASSOVER CUSHION CASES

Jews are commanded to 'lean' during the Seder service to demonstrate that they are free. This custom probably dates from Roman times when the guests at banquets reclined on couches. Over the ages it has been customary to embroider pillow cases or cushion covers specifically for this purpose.

THE MEGILLAH COVER

The Torah is written upon a scroll (page 86); there are also other scrolls which are used for special festivals during the year. The story of Esther is read in the synagogue during the festival of Purim, from a special small scroll known as the *megillat Esther*. The Torah scroll has two rollers, one at each end, but the megillat Esther has only one.

Megillot Esther are owned by the synagogue and also by private individuals. In the past it was customary in some countries for a megillat Esther to

Fig. 108 *Passover pillowcase; silk embroidery upon silk, one of a set embroidered with the five expressions of redemption which were promised, as written in Exodus. Isaac Sassoon, London. (Private collection.)*

Fig. 109 *Antique megillah with a megillah cover by Naomi Cohen-Ziv, London. Silk, leather, gold thread, beads and sequins.*

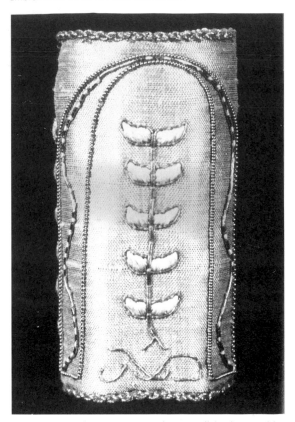

Fig. 110 *Cover for an antique Italian megillah, designed by Kathryn Salomon and embroidered by Caroline Lee. Silk and metal-thread embroidery upon silk. 9 × 10.5 cm (3½ × 4 in.). (Private collection.)*

be given as a wedding present from the bride to the groom. The megillah is written in a special script, just as the Torah is, but there is a difference. The Torah is never illuminated but many megillot Esther have been beautifully decorated. In the past, exquisite silver cases were sometimes used for the megillot and embroidered covers were also used.

Figure *110* shows a cover for a megillat Esther which I designed and Caroline Lee embroidered. The antique megillah for which it was made came from Italy and was illuminated. The owner of the megillah wished the embroidery to reflect the illumination and so I took some of the decorative details and manipulated them to create an original design.

There is no specific symbolism for a megillah

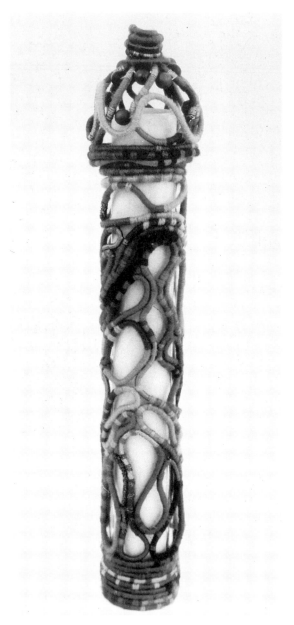

Fig. 111 *Megillah cover by Ina Golub, Mountainside, New Jersey; fibre filigree, mixed fibres. 54 × 8 cm (21 × 3 in.)*

cover. Purim is a time of festivity and jollity, so one could use that theme. Figure *109* shows a cover by Naomi Cohen-Ziv in which Queen Esther is depicted.

chapter twelve

The mizrach and shevitti and the mezuzah

THE MIZRACH AND THE SHEVITI

Jews face the east for prayer and this has led to a special folk custom which became popular in the

Fig. 112 *Mizrach by Estelle Levy, London.*

eighteenth and nineteenth centuries. Panels were made to hang on the eastern wall of the home, to indicate the direction for prayer. They contained the word *mizrach* which means 'east' and sometimes contained biblical verses. They were decorated with

pictures of Jerusalem and designs which might contain flowers and animals. They could be drawings on paper, papercuts, etchings on copper, prints, or embroidered panels.

Some orthodox homes today still use a mizrach, and they can also be found in synagogues when

Fig. 113 *Mezuzah case by Linda Price, Manchester. Hand and machine embroidery worked into leather which was then stretched and glued on to a wooden block.*

Fig. 114 *Mezuzah case, Morocco, nineteenth century. Silver-gilt thread on velvet. (Israel Museum, Jerusalem.)*

Fig. 115 *Mezuzah case, Algeria, end of the nineteenth century. Silver thread on velvet. (Israel Museum, Jerusalem.)*

daily prayers are said in a small room rather than the prayer hall.

A mizrach is essentially a picture and can be an embroidered panel. Any materials can be used and the choice of symbolism is very free. As in so many other Jewish items, the Hebrew script is so pleasing that the word 'mizrach' alone can form a beautiful decoration.

Sheviti are devotional panels which include biblical phrases or quotations from the Psalms. They were and are made in exactly the same way as a mizrach.

THE MEZUZAH

Deuteronomy 6:4–9 and 11:13–21 contain the fundamental precepts of Judaism and form one of the most important prayers, the Shema, which is recited daily. This passage contains the injunction to put the prayer 'upon the doorposts of thy house'. It is for this reason that we affix a *mezuzah* (which means doorpost) on the doorposts of our houses.

The mezuzah consists of a piece of parchment with the passages from Deuteronomy mentioned above hand-written upon it. Franz Landsberger has described how early mezuzot probably consisted of the rolled-up parchment placed in a niche in the doorpost. In time a container was used to keep the parchment clean and dry. A hollow reed was probably used first and later more elaborate cases were developed. Mention of glass tubes can be found from the seventeenth century, and in the eighteenth century wealthy patrons commissioned elaborate silver cases. In the West, wood and other hard materials were also used, but a different custom developed in North Africa. Jews in Morocco used flat, embroidered cases which look like pockets or badges. They were decorated with hearts, shields, stars and hands with all the fingers open, as well as other symbols. The word 'Shaddai' (Almighty) and the name of the embroiderer or the recipient were also included. In some places it was the custom for the bride to bring an embroidered mezuzah to her new home.

Some modern embroiderers have looked at the mezuzah as an article to be developed as a piece of embroidery. This is certainly an area worth considering.

chapter thirteen

Hebrew lettering

The Hebrew alphabet consists of 22 letters and is usually written without vowels. It developed from the Phoenician script. Originally, the letters were first written upon a stone with a reed, and then chiselled out. The easiest way to carve the letters, if the craftsman held the mallet in his left hand and the chisel in his right, would have been from right to left. Hebrew has retained this characteristic and is written from right to left.

During the thousands of years in which the Jews have lived in the Diaspora, the script has taken on different characteristics according to where the Jews were living. Oriental and Sephardi scribes usually used a reed pen, and their letters are softer and rounder than the Ashkenazi script. Ashkenazi and Italian scribes used a feather quill pen which also affected the formation of the letters. The various scripts have taken on some of the characteristics of the dominant culture amongst which the Jews were living. Thus certain qualities of Arabic or Latin lettering can be discerned in the Hebrew script from different areas.

The embroiderer can study different styles of Hebrew lettering from a number of sources. Hebrew illuminated manuscripts reveal beautiful alphabets.

Fig. 116 *Torah mantle for the High Holy Days designed by Rabbi Reinhart and worked by Beryl Dean MBE. Oyster-coloured satin with d'Alençon lace, satin stitch in a self colour. The lettering includes the 'tagin' – small, crown-like* motifs which are always used on specific letters when a scribe writes a Torah scroll, mezzuzah or megillah. (Westminster Synagogue, London.)

It is interesting to note that as Hebrew script does not use capital letters, the custom of enlarging and decorating the initial letter as in Christian illuminated manuscripts is rarely employed. Instead, the practice of enlarging the whole of the initial word into a decorative panel evolved.

The Torah scroll, the megillot and mezzuzot are all written with a special script. An example of this style of lettering can be seen on the Torah mantle embroidered by Beryl Dean and designed by Rabbi Reinhart (fig. 116). Note the three little lines which form a crown and appear over some of the letters. They are known as *tagin* and are only used on the following letters:

$$שעטנזגצ$$

Another form of Jewish letter decoration is micrography, the use of minute script to form pictures. This custom was used by Jewish scribes in the early Muslim period and was taken by them to Christian Europe. The Muslim-influenced designs are mainly floral or geometric whilst the Christian-influenced designs include animal and human figures.

diagram 69 *A Hebrew letter manipulated to form a deer. From an eighteenth century binder in the collection of the Jewish Museum, London.*

diagram 68 *A Hebrew letter manipulated to form a stork. From an eighteenth century binder in the collection of the Jewish Museum, London.*

145

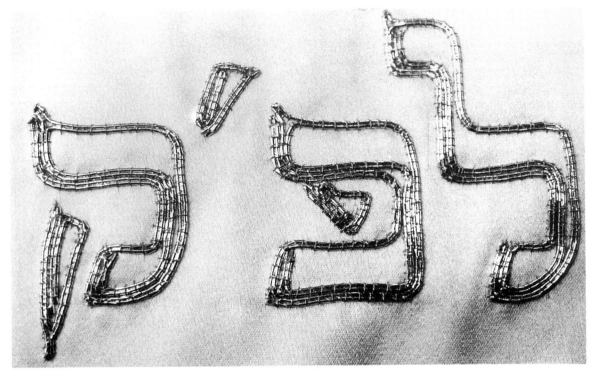

Fig. 117 *Hebrew lettering by Millie Jaffé. Couched in Jap gold.*

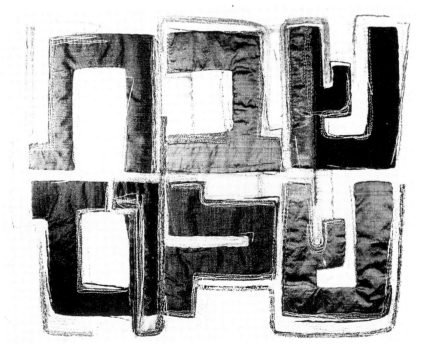

Fig. 118 *Challah cover by Kathryn Salomon: silk with silk appliqué, machine and hand stitchery. The words 'Shabbat Shalom' welcome the Sabbath.*

146

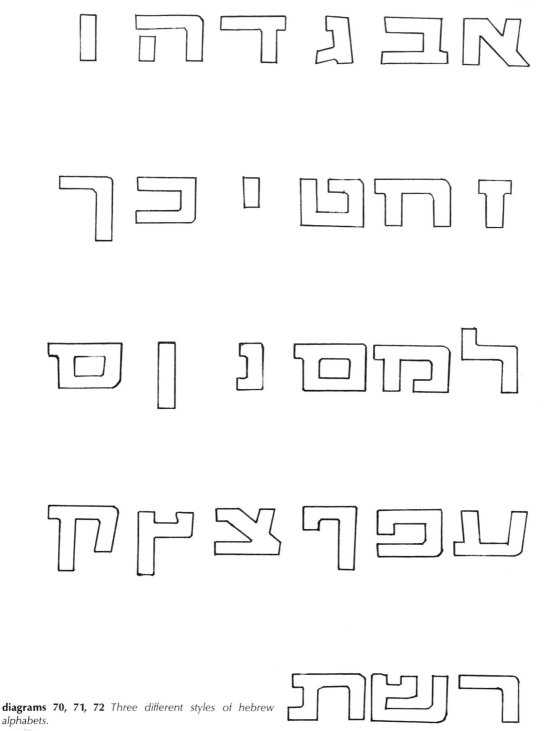

diagrams 70, 71, 72 *Three different styles of hebrew alphabets.*

א ב ג ד ה ו

ז ח ט י כ ך

ל מ ם נ ן ס ע פ

ע פ ף צ ץ ק

ר ש ת

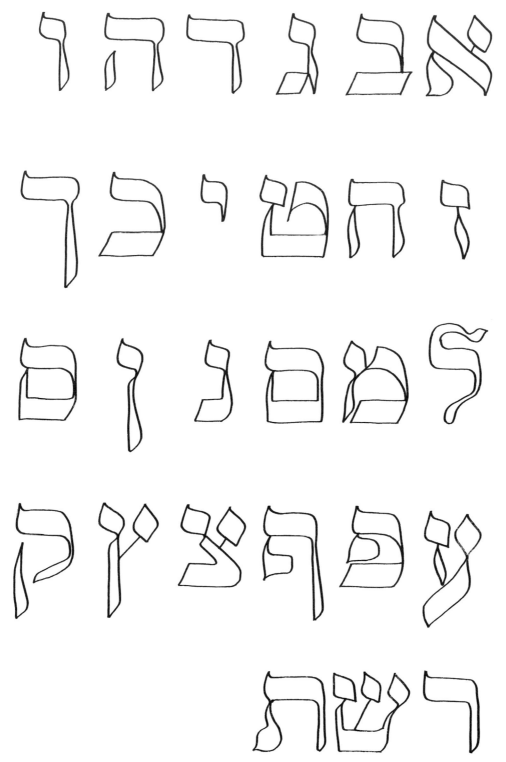

diagram 73 *The development of the design for the 'Living Water' Torah mantle. The Hebrew word for life was gradually distorted to form a flowing design.*

Torah binders show the very decorative way letters have been embellished by embroiderers in the past. Scribes were frequently asked to write the lettering on the fabric for the embroiderers and contemporary styles of illumination can be followed on the binders. As in illuminated manuscripts, letters were made of animal and human forms, sometimes creating fantastic creatures. The serifs in some of the binders were developed into flowers and tendrils.

A modern source of a variety of styles of lettering can be found in dry transfer alphabets. A number of different styles can be purchased; you can see examples of some of them on the preceding pages.

LETTERING IN DEDICATIONS

Many Jewish items contain a dedicatory inscription. Obviously the wording needs to be clear and legible. Clarity rather than aesthetic considerations is the most important element.

LETTERING IN DESIGN

Legibility may be a disadvantage when lettering is used for design purposes. If the eye is immediately drawn to read the words, the design element can be destroyed. It is very hard to keep the two different factors in one's mind at the same time. It is like drawing a trick picture which can be two totally different things; you can see one and then the other, but never both at the same time. Often designers deliberately use incomplete words or a jumbled mixture of letters so that the words are not instantly legible.

It may be that it is the general unfamiliarity with the Hebrew alphabet which allows us to see how decorative it is. We can appreciate the shape of the letters because so many of us have difficulty in reading them! (This is also true of other scripts such as Greek, Russian or Arabic, with which many of us are unfamiliar.)

Figs. 119, 120 *Two different methods of working Hebrew lettering.*

Appendix:
storage of synagogue vestments

Every synagogue uses at least two sets of vestments, one for the majority of the year and one for the High Holy Days. Items for the High Holy Days will be stored for all but ten days of the year and the other vestments will be stored during the High Holy Day period. There are some synagogues which use different coloured vestments for the festivals and so have more items to store.

Fig. 121 *An efficient method of storing parochot. They are hung one in front of the other on steel poles which are raised and lowered by means of pulleys.*

It is no use the embroiderer assuming that the synagogue officials will know how to store embroideries. In the majority of cases they will have no idea, and the storage may be handled by a succession of voluntary officials, with no one bearing the responsibility if any item is damaged. The problem really needs to be investigated by the embroiderer and a solution found and suggested to the synagogue when the vestments are presented.

It is worth pointing out to the officials that vestments will last much longer and be more cost-effective if they are stored properly.

Parochot

Parochot are large items and need careful storage. The problem is greater if a synagogue possesses a number of parochot for different occasions. A particular synagogue with six Ark curtains copes with the storage problem in the following manner:

The curtain for Shabbat and the one for the weekdays are hung, one in front of the other, in front of the Ark. There is a cord for each curtain, one each side of the Ark. When the Shabbat curtain is in use, the weekday curtain is pulled to one side. During the week the Shabbat curtain hangs behind the weekday curtain. The other parochot are stored in a basement storeroom, one in front of the other, hung from steel poles. The poles are raised and lowered by means of pulleys when the curtains need to be removed.

Torah mantles

Whenever possible mantles should be stored covered with a fabric covering to keep off the dust. The best method is for the mantles to be kept upon stands constructed for the purpose as then there is no strain on any part of the mantle and they are not creased. Unfortunately, all too often space is a problem and there is no room for this method. The alternative is to hang the mantles by means of string passed between the two holes of the hard tops. Storing the mantles in a box is not to be recommended. Creases will inevitably be formed because of the hard top, and the mantles will suffer.

Glossary

Aron, Aron ha-Kodesh: the Holy Ark. The receptacle in which the sifrei Torah, the scrolls of the Law, are kept.

Ashkenazim: Jews of Central and Eastern European origins.

Atarah: decorated textile piece sewn to that part of the prayer shawl which touches the neck. Also used for Crown of the Law; see *Keter*.

Barmitzvah: 'Son of the commandment'. The ceremony which a Jewish boy undergoes at the age of 13 when he is considered morally responsible for his own actions.

Batmitzvah: 'Daughter of the commandment'. The same ceremony as above, but performed by a girl. Only performed in Progressive synagogues.

BCE: Before the Common Era.

Bimah: the Ashkenazi term for the raised platform on which the reader's desk stands and from which the Torah is read.

B'nei Torah: 'Sons or children of the Law'. A ceremony performed by older youths, or girls in Progressive synagogues, celebrating their commitment to Judaism.

CE: Common Era.

Challah, pl. challot: plaited bread which is eaten on Shabbat and festivals.

Cherubim (sing. cherub): the fantastic creatures, made of four different types of animals, which were above the altar in the Sanctuary and the Temple.

Chuppah: wedding canopy.

Etrog: citrus fruit (citrus medica).

Etzei Hayim (sing. Etz Hayim): 'Trees of Life'. The rods which support each end of the Torah scroll. (The Torah is referred to as a Tree of Life in Proverbs 3:18.)

Haggadah: prayer book for the Seder service.

Kapporet: valance for the Torah Ark.

Keter: crown of the Law; a silver or silver-gilt ornament for the Torah scroll.

Kiddush: prayer of sanctification, recited over a cup of wine on Sabbaths and festivals.

Kippah: yarmulke, skullcap.

Lulav: literally 'palm branch' but used to describe the bundle of palm shoots, myrtle twigs and willow branches used during the festival of Succot (Tabernacles).

Matzah, pl. matzot: unleavened bread, eaten on Passover (Pesach).

Megillah: a scroll, usually parchment. The megillat Esther is the story of Esther which is read in the synagogue on the festival of Purim. It has one roller as opposed to the Torah scroll which has two.

Menorah: seven-branched candlestick, mentioned in Exodus 25:31–6.

Mezuzah: 'doorpost'. The mezuzah is the text of Deuteronomy 6:4–9 and 11:13–21, written by a scribe upon a piece of parchment. The word Shaddai (Almighty) is written upon the back so that it can be seen when the mezuzah is placed in a case and fixed to the doorpost.

Mizrach: literally 'east'; a panel, picture or sign which is placed on the eastern wall to indicate the direction for prayer.

Parokhet (pl. parochot): curtain for the Torah Ark.

Pesach: Passover.

Purim: the Feast of Lots. Minor holiday upon which the megillat Esther is read.

Rimmonim: the Torah finials.

Romaniot: Jews who trace their ancestry back to Alexandria in the Babylonian Diaspora.

Rosh ha-Shanah: the New Year.

Seder: literally 'Order'. A special service and meal on the Eve of the Passover which takes place in the home.

Sephardim: Jews who trace their ancestry back to Spain and Portugal. They were expelled from Spain in the fifteenth century.

Shabbat: Sabbath.

Shavuot: Pentecost.

Shofar: ram's horn, blown on the New Year and Day of Atonement.

Sukkot: Feast of Tabernacles.

Tallit, pl. tallitot: prayer shawl.

Talmud: Rabbinic commentaries upon the Torah which were first oral and then written down between 200 and 500 CE.

Teffilin: phylacteries.

Torah: the Law – the five books of Moses: Genesis, Exodus, Leviticus, Numbers and Deuteronomy. They are written upon a parchment scroll and a portion is read on weekdays, Shabbat and festivals.

Tik: cylindrical case for the Torah scroll used by Romaniote Jews. Generally wood, sometimes overlaid with precious metal. Known from the tenth century in Iraq.

Tzitzit: ritual fringes attached to the four corners of the tallit.

Yom Kippur: Day of Atonement. The holiest day in the Jewish year when Jews fast for 25 hours and make atonement for the sins of the past year.

Selected bibliography

Aber, Ita, *The Art of Judaic Needlework*, Bell and Hyman, London, in association with Charles Scribners Sons, New York.

Abrahams, I., *Jewish Life in the Middle Ages*, Jewish Publication Society of America, Philadelphia, 1960.

Beese, Pat, *Embroidery for the Church*, Studio Vista, 1975.

Bialer, Yehuda L., *Jewish Life in Art and Tradition*, Putmans, New York, Wiedenfeld and Nicolson, London, 1976.

Dawson, Barbara, *Metal Thread Embroidery*, Batsford, 1968.

Dean, Beryl, *Embroidery in Religion and Ceremonial*, Batsford, 1981.

Dodwell, C. R., ed., *Jewish Art Treasures from Prague*, Lund Humphries, London, in association with the Whitworth Gallery, 1980.

Encylopaedia Judaica, Keter, Jerusalem, 1972.

Eis, Ruth, *Torah Binders of the Judah L. Magnes Museum*, 1979.

Eis, Ruth, *Ornamented Bags for Tallit and Teffilin of the Judah L. Magnes Museum*, 1984.

Fishburn, Angela, *The Batsford Book of Soft Furnishings*, Batsford, 1978.

Freehof, Lillian S. and Bucky King, *Embroideries and Fabrics for Synagogue and Home*, Hearthside Press Inc. New York, 1966.

Goodman, Hanna and Goodman, Philip, *The Jewish Marriage Anthology*, Jewish Publication Society of America, Philadelphia, 1965.

Goodman, Philip, *The Passover Anthology*, Jewish Publication Society of America, Philadelphia, 1966.

Goodenough, Irwin, *Jewish Symbols of the Greco-Roman Period*, Vols. 9–11, Princeton University Press, 1954.

Gutman, Joseph, ed., *Beauty in Holiness*, Ktav Publishing Inc., 1970.

Gutman, Joseph, *No Graven Image*, Ktav Publishing Inc., 1971.

Grimwade, A. G., and Barnett, R. D., *Treasures of a London Temple*, Taylors Foreign Press, 1951.

Jewish Encyclopaedia, Funk and Wagnalls, New York and London, 1905 and subsequent editions.

Journal of Jewish Art, Spertus College of Judaica Press. A number of interesting articles related to embroidery in different volumes.

Kamf, Avram, *Contemporary Synagogue Art*, Union of American Hebrew Congregations, New York, 1966.

Kanof, Abram, *Jewish Ceremonial Art and Religious Observance*, Abrams, New York.

Kayser, Stephen S., and Schoenberger, Guido, eds., *Jewish Ceremonial Art*, Jewish Publication Society of America, Philadelphia, 1959.

Kirshenblatt-Gimblett, and Grossman, Cissy, *Fabric of Jewish Life: Textiles from the Jewish Museum Collection*, Jewish Museum, New York, 1977.

Lemon, Jane, *A Dictionary of Metal Thread Embroidery*, Batsford, 1987.

Narkiss, Bezalel, *Hebrew Illuminated Manuscripts*, New York, 1969.

Roth, Cecil, ed., revised by Narkiss, Bezalel, *Jewish Art, An Illustrated History*, Vallentine Mitchell, London, 1971.

Russell, Pat, *Lettering for Embroidery*, Batsford, reprint 1985.

Segal, Richard, Strassfeld, Michael and Strassfeld, Sharon, *First Jewish Catalog*, The Jewish Publication Society of America, Philadelphia, 1973.

Shafter Rockland, Mae, *The Work of Our Hands, Jewish Needlework for Today*, Schocken Books, New York, 1973.

Selected bibliography

State Jewish Museum, Prague, *Torah Binders from Four Centuries*.

Volovakova, Hana, *The Synagogue Treasures of Bohemia and Moravia*, Sfinz, Prague, 1949.

Wischnitzer, Mark, *A History of Jewish Crafts and Guilds*, Jonathan David, New York, 1965.

Witschnitzer, Rachel, *The Art and Architecture of the European Synagogue*, Jewish Publication Society of America, Philadelphia, 1964.

Witschnitzer, Rachel, 'Art', in: Finkelstein, Louis, ed., *The Jews, Their History, Culture and Religion*, Peter Owen, London, 1961.

Yeshiva University Museum, *Tradition and Fantasy in Jewish Needlework*, Catalogue of an exhibition, November 1981–June 1982.

Useful addresses

The *Jewish Travel Guide*, published annually by the *Jewish Chronicle*, London (25 Furnival Street, London EC4) lists names and addresses of synagogues and places of Jewish interest worldwide. Another useful source is: Abramson, Samuel H., and Postal, Bernard, *The Traveler's Guide to Jewish Landmarks of Europe*, Fleet Press Corp., New York, 1971.

BRITAIN

Museums

Jewish Museum
Woburn House
Upper Woburn Place
London WC1H 0EP

Manchester Jewish Museum
190 Cheetham Hill Road
Manchester M8 8LW

London Museum of Jewish Life
(Incorporates Museum of the Jewish East End)
Sternberg Centre for Judaism
80 East End Road
London N3 2SY

Victoria and Albert Museum
South Kensington
London SW7 2RL
Many items of Jewish interest are not on permanent display but can be viewed by appointment.

Synagogues

Please never visit a synagogue to see the embroideries without first making an appointment with the secretary. Many items will be stored for special times of the year and will not be easily accessible. Some synagogues are reluctant to be listed as unexpected visitors can be such a problem. It will help all embroiderers to see more work if everyone is co-operative and makes an appointment.

Liberal Jewish Synagogue
28 St John's Wood Road
London NW8

New North London Synagogue
80 East End Road
London N3 2SY

North Western Reform Synagogue
Alyth Gardens
London NW11

New West End Synagogue
10 St Petersberg Place
London W2

Spanish and Portuguese Jews Congregation
Maida Vale
London
(01-289 2573)

Westminster Synagogue
Kent House
Rutland Gardens
London SW7

Yeshurun Hebrew Congregation
Coniston Road
Gatley
Cheshire S8 4AP

UNITED STATES

Museums
American Jewish Historical Society
2 Thornton Road
Walton
Massachusetts 02154

B'nai B'rith Klutznick Museum
1640 Rhode Island Avenue NW
Washington DC 20036

Congregation Emanu-El
1 East 65th Street
New York
NY 10021

HUC Skirball Museum
3077 University Avenue
Los Angeles
California 90007-3796

International Synagogue
J.F.K. International Airport
Jamaica
New York
NY 11430

Jewish Museum
1109 5th Avenue
New York
NY 10028

Jewish Community Museum
121 Steuart Street
San Francisco
CA 94105

Judah L. Magnes Museum
2911 Russell Street
Berkeley
CA 94705

National Museum of American Jewish History
Independence Mall East
55 N 5th Street
Philadelphia
Penn 19106

The Temple
University Circle at Silver Park
Cleveland
Ohio 44106

Temple Emanu-El Museum
99 Taft Avenue
Providence
Rhode Island 02906

The Temple Judea Museum of Kneseth Israel
York Road and Township Line
Elkins Park
PA 19117

Wilshire Boulevard Temple
Edgar F. Magnin Square
3663 Wilshire Boulevard
Los Angeles
CA 90010

There are so many synagogues in the United States and Canada which possess fine modern embroideries that it is impossible to list them. Some may be found by looking at the captions of the illustrations.

Publications and groups
Pomegranate Guild of Judaic Needlework
PO Box 4150
Great Neck
New York
NY 11027

EUROPE

Many capital cities and places which have had large Jewish populations in the past have Jewish museums and the embroiderer should consult *The Jewish Travel Guide* or the local tourist office. A few museums are listed below:

Jewish Museum Amsterdam
Oudespiegelstraat 7
Amsterdam 101 6BM
Holland

Jewish Museum of Greece
36 Amalias Avenue
10058 Athens
Greece

Jewish Museum Rome
Lungotevere
Cenci 9
Rome
Italy

Jewish Museum
Communita Israelitica de Venezia
Ghetto Vecchio 1188/A
Venice
Italy

Verein für das Judische Museum der Schweiz
Kornhausgasse 8
4051 Basel
Switzerland

State Jewish Museum
110 01 Prague 1
Jachymova 3
Czechoslovakia

Israel
The Israel Museum
Jerusalem

Italian Jewry Museum
27 Hillel St
Jerusalem

Sir Isaac and Lady Edith Wolfson Museum
Hechal Shlomo
58 King George Street
Jerusalem

INFORMATION

The Centre for Jewish Art is producing an index of all Judaica from all over the world. This is available to both professional and lay people. There is a survey of items in the possession of synagogues from Iran, Iraq, India, Libya, Tunis, Morroco, Greece and Turkey. It is organized into a card index with detailed descriptions and photographs. The Centre for Jewish Art can be contacted at:

The Centre for Jewish Art
POB 4262
Jerusalem 90142

Suppliers

BRITAIN

Aisenthal, J.
11 Ashbourne Parade
Finchley Road
London NW11
Tzitzit, mezzuzot

Allans
55–6 Duke Street
London W1M 6HS
Fine fabrics

Borovick Fabrics Ltd
16 Berwick Street
London W1V 4HP

de Denne Ltd
159–161 Kenton Road
Kenton
Harrow
Middlesex
General embroidery supplies

Ells and Farrier Ltd
20 Princes Street
London W1
Beads

Embroiderers' Guild
Apartment 41
Hampton Court Palace
East Molesey
Surrey KR8 9AU
Books and information for members

Harrods Ltd
London SW1
Furnishing fabrics, velvets

John Lewis Partnership
Oxford Street
London W1S 1EX
General haberdashery, linings, interlinings, calico, some silks

Mace & Nairn
89 Crane Street
Salisbury
Wiltshire SP1 2PY
Metal threads and general embroidery materials

Manor House Book Service
80 East End Road
London N3
Tzitzit, mezuzot

Liberty & Co plc
Regent Street
London W1
Silk fabrics and fabrics

Royal School of Needlework
25 Princes Gate
Kensington, London SW7 1QE
Metal threads and general embroidery supplies

Shirley Institute
Didsbury
Manchester
061 445 8141
Professional testing house and advice service for textiles

Stephen Simpson Ltd
Avenham Road Works
Preston
Lurex threads and cords, copper threads, gilt metal threads

Vilene Organisation
PO Box 3
Ellistone Lane
Greetland
Halifax
West Yorks HX4 8NJ
Advice on different weights and types of Vilene interfacing

Watts & Co Ltd
7 Tufton Street
London SW1
Church furnishers; specialist fabrics, braids and cords

Wippell & Co Ltd
11 Tufton Street
London SW1
Church furnishers

Wippell & Co Ltd
POB 1
88 Buller Road
St Thomas Street
Exeter
Devon EX4 1DQ

Wippell & Co Ltd
24 King Street
Manchester

Whaleys (Bradford) Ltd
Harris Court
Great Horton
Bradford
West Yorkshire
Silk, cotton and woollen fabric for dyeing and printing, vanishing muslin

UNITED STATES

Britex Fabrics
146 Geary
San Francisco
CA 94108
Fabrics, braids etc.

Exotic Thai Silks
252 State St
Los Altos
CA 94022
Silks from China, Thailand, India, etc. Mail order

Far Eastern Fabrics
171 Madison Avenue
New York
NY 10016
Wholesale silks (minimum quantity 3 yards of one colour)

G. Street Fabrics
11854 Rockville Pike
Rockville
MD 20852
Mail order, retail, fabrics

Jack Lenor Larsen
232 East 59th St
New York
NY 10022
Wholesale only, minimum 2 yards, fine upholstery-weight fabrics

The Needle's Point Studio
216 Appleblossom Court
Vienna
Virginia 22180
General embroidery supplies

Pellon Corporation
119 West 40th St
New York
NY 10018
Advice on different weights and types of Pellon interfacing

Tinsel Trading Co
47 West 38th Street
New York
NY 10018
Metal threads, all qualities, some mail order

Wippell & Co Ltd
59 Willet St
POB 1696
Bloomfield
NJ 07001
Church furnishers

Index

Page references in italics indicate illustrations, and those in bold indicate that text and illustrations occur on the same page.